HEINEMANN HISTORY

STUDY UNITS

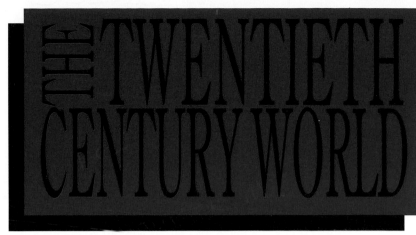

THE TWENTIETH CENTURY WORLD

Nigel Kelly
Martyn Whittock

Heinemann Library,
a division of Heinemann Publishers (Oxford) Ltd,
Halley Court, Jordan Hill, Oxford OX2 8EJ

OXFORD LONDON EDINBURGH MADRID
ATHENS BOLOGNA PARIS MELBOURNE
SYDNEY AUCKLAND SINGAPORE TOKYO
IBADAN NAIROBI HARARE GABORONE
PORTSMOUTH NH (USA)

First published 1993

This edition published 1995

95 96 97 98 10 9 8 7 6 5 4 3 2 1

**British Library Cataloguing in Publication Data is available
from the British Library on request.**

ISBN 0–431–07363–5

Designed by Ron Kamen, Green Door Design Ltd, Basingstoke

Illustrated by Phill Burrows, Jeff Edwards and Andrew
Greenwood

Printed in Hong Kong

The front cover shows a still from 'The Great Dictator'

Acknowledgements

The author and publisher would like to thank the following for
permission to reproduce photographs:
AKG London: 3.7C, 3.7I, 3.7H; Bildarchiv Preussischer
Kulturbesitz: 3.7R; Bilderdienst Suddeutscher Verlag: 4.8D;
Bildergenbur Schuster / Dr Müller: 6.1B; Bridgeman Art Library:
3.1C; Bridgeman Art Library / Imperial War Museum: 2.3E,
2.3H, 2.3L; British Library: 2.4A; Bundesarchiv, Koblenz: 3.7T,
3.7V; Collins Educational: 5.2A; E. T. Archives: 4.8A, 4.9Z;
Mary Evans Picture Library: 1.1C, 4.9V; Gunn Brinson: 3.7Q;
Robert Harding Picture Library: 6.1F; Robert Harding Picture
Library / Glyn Genin: 6.1A; Robert Harding Picture Library /
David Lomax: 6.1E; Hulton Deutsch Collection: 2.3C, 2.3N,
3.4E, 4.9C, 4.9U; Robert Hunt Library: 2.1B; Imperial War
Museum: 2.3B, 2.3S, 3.6A, 4.1A, 4.3B, 4.5A, 4.8H, 4.9E, 4.9M,
4.9R; International Ladies Garment Workers' Union Archives /
Labor-Management Documentation Center, Cornell University:
3.7O; David King Collection: 5.5C; David Low / Evening
Standard / Centre for the Study of Cartoons and Caricature,
University of Kent at Canterbury / Solo Syndication & Literary
Agency Ltd: 3.7L; National Air and Space Museum,
Smithsonion Institution: 4.7D; Netherlands Photo Archive /
Charles Breijer: 4.4C; Popperfoto: 3.4A, 3.7S, 4.9E, 4.9P, 5.1D;
Topham Picturepoint: Cover, 3.7G, 4.2A, 5.6D; Weimar
Archive: 3.7O, 4.6B

Every effort has been made to contact copyright holders of
material published in this book. Any omissions will be rectified
in subsequent printings if notice is given to the publisher.

Thanks to Dr Harriet Jones for her comments on the original
manuscript.

*To my good friend and first head of history, Steven Tamplin, Queen
Elizabeth's School, Wimborne, Dorset. MW.*

Details of written sources

In some sources the wording or sentence structure has been
simplified to ensure that the source is accessible.
BBC, *The Complete Blackadder Goes Forth*, BBC Videos, 1992:
2.1A
Malcolm Brown, *Tommy Goes to War*, J. M. Dent, 1972: 2.2B,
2.3B, 2.3A, 2.3D, 2.3G, 2.3K, 2.3O, 2.3Q, 2.3P, 2.3Y
S. L. Case, *The Second World War*, Evans Brothers, 1981: 4.6A
Brian Catchpole, *A Map History of the Modern World*,
Heinemann, 1982: 3.2A, 3.3A, 5.3F
Margaret Costa, 'Reliving 1946: The Food Front', *Sunday Times*, 2
May 1965: 4.9S
Chris Culpin, *Making History: World History from 1914 to the
Present Day*, Collins, 1986: 4.9W
N. DeMarco, *The World this Century*, Unwin Hyman, 1987: 5.5B
B. Eliott, *Hitler and Germany*, Longman, 1966: 3.2B
J. Fest, *The Face of the Third Reich*, Pelican, 1984: 3.7J
P. Fisher, *The Great Power Conflict after 1945*, Simon and
Schuster, 1993: 5.6A, 5.6B
P. Fisher and N. Williams, *Past into Present, Book 3*, Collins, 1988:
3.4B
History of the Second World War, Purnell, 1968: 3.5B, 4.7B
Tony Howarth, *Twentieth Century History: The World Since 1900*,
Longman, 1979: 3.6C, 4.8E
F. Judd, *The Brandt Report: Stalemate at Cancun - Where do we go
from here?*, Geobooks in association with the University College
of Swansea, 1982: 6.1D
Nigel Kelly, *The First World War*, Heinemann, 1989: 2.2A, 2.3A,
2.3F, 2.3T, 2.3W
Nigel Kelly, *The Second World War*, Heinemann, 1989: 3.3B, 4.5B,
4.7C, 4.8B, 4.8C, 4.8G, 4.9A, 5.3E
Stephen Lee, *Nazi Germany*, Heinemann, 1989: 3.4D, 3.5E,
3.7M, 4.9Y
C. K. McDonald, *The Second World War*, Blackwell, 1984: 4.7A,
4.9T
P. Mantin, *The Twentieth Century World*, Hutchinson, 1987: 3.9J,
4.3F
Peter Moss, *Modern World History*, Hart-Davis, 1978: 5.2C
Novosti Press Agency, *Recalling the Past*, Moscow, 1985: 3.5G
H. L. Peacock, *A History of Modern Europe 1789–1981*,
Heinemann, 1982: 1.1B
Alistair and Anne Pike, *The Home Front: Oral and Contemporary
Accounts*, Tressel, 1985: 4.9L, 4.9N
R. Rees, *Britain and the Great War*, Heinemann, 1993: 2.3J, 2.3R
J. Roberts (Ed), *History of the Twentieth Century*, Purnell, 1968:
5.4B
J. Roberts, *History of the World*, Pelican, 1980: 3.2C
Joe Scott, *The World Since 1914*, Heinemann, 1989: 4.3A, 5.1B,
5.2D
R. Seth, *Operation Barbarossa*, Blond, 1964: 4.2B
K. Shephard, *International Relations 1919–39*, Blackwell, 1987:
3.6E, 3.6F
J. Simpkin, *Contemporary Account of the Second World War*,
Tressell, 1984: 4.4A, 4.4B, 4.8I, 4.9G
L. E. Snellgrove, *The Modern World Since 1870*, Longman, 1981:
2.5B, 3.4C, 3.5F, 5.1C
Norman Stone, *Hitler*, Coronet Books, 1980: 3.7U
T. Walter Wallbank, *Contemporary Africa: Continent in Transition*,
Van Nostrand, 1964: 5.4C
Ben Wicks, *No Time to Wave Goodbye*, Bloomsbury, 1988: 4.9O,
4.9Q
B. York, *The Soviet Union 1917–80*, Nelson, 1983: 3.1A

CONTENTS

1.1 The Twentieth Century – An Overview

Perhaps more than any other century, the 20th century has been one of conflict. There has been conflict between countries and also between people within individual countries.

The First World War and its consequences

At the beginning of the century rivalry between the European powers split the continent into two armed camps, the **Triple Entente** (Britain, France and Russia) and the **Triple Alliance** (Germany, Austria-Hungary and Italy). This rivalry led to the First World War (1914–18) with its twenty million military and civilian deaths. The high casualty figures reflected a new kind of war, 'total war'. Technological advances meant that from now on warfare was not limited just to the battlefield, but also had a direct effect on the daily lives of civilians at home. When peace came in 1918 the victorious powers blamed the war on Germany. Severe penalties were placed on Germany by the **Treaty of Versailles.**

'The war to end all wars'. It was scenes like this which convinced people in 1918 that there could never be another war like the First World War.

A

SOURCE

From peace to war

In 1919, the **League of Nations** was set up to help maintain peace and ensure that disputes between countries would be settled by discussion and not by resorting to war. By this time important changes were taking place.

The greatest change occurred in Russia. In the **Russian Revolution** of 1917 **Tsar Nicholas II** was overthrown and a communist government took control. Russia was later renamed the **Union of Soviet Socialist Republics**. The communists did not like a small number of rich businessmen controlling the country's wealth. They believed that workers should rise up and overthrow the rich people. The government should then run the country for the benefit of all, rather than allowing individuals to make private profit. Communism was an attractive idea to some other countries, but it was fiercely resisted by politicians in the USA and Western Europe. To them communism was a threat to all they believed in and would lead to chaos if it took a hold in their own country. For this reason it was often stamped out with great severity.

In 1922 **Benito Mussolini** seized power in Italy. He turned Italy into a **fascist dictatorship**. In 1933 the Nazi Party, led by **Adolf Hitler**, came to power in Germany. Soon the Nazis had total control over the lives of the German people. Both Mussolini and Hitler used armed forces to take over other countries. It was no surprise when, in 1936, Germany and Italy became allies.

Unfortunately, the League of Nations had a number of in-built weaknesses and was unable to deal with a number of threats to world peace in the 1930s. First Japan, then Italy and finally Germany carried out attacks on other countries in a bid to get more land and become more powerful. Each time the League's actions had no effect. The harshness of the Treaty of Versailles made the German people so bitter that some historians believe Germany was bound to seek

B

SOURCE

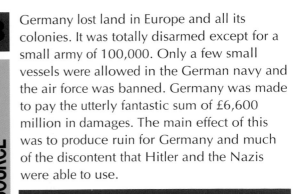

Germany lost land in Europe and all its colonies. It was totally disarmed except for a small army of 100,000. Only a few small vessels were allowed in the German navy and the air force was banned. Germany was made to pay the utterly fantastic sum of £6,600 million in damages. The main effect of this was to produce ruin for Germany and much of the discontent that Hitler and the Nazis were able to use.

H. L. Peacock commenting on the Treaty of Versailles in 'A History of Modern Europe 1789–1981', 1982.

C

SOURCE

The front cover of an Italian newspaper showing Hitler and Mussolini at a parade in Berlin in 1937.

revenge for its defeat in 1918. So it proved when German invaded Poland in 1939 and the **Second World War** broke out.

The Second World War

The first two years of the Second World War (1939–45) saw Hitler win control of almost all of Europe. At the end of 1940 only Britain stood between Nazi Germany and victory. However, in 1941 Hitler invaded the USSR and his ally, Japan, attacked the American base of **Pearl Harbor** as part of its plan to build an empire in the Pacific. Thus, the war developed into a world-wide conflict which killed 55 million people – half of whom were civilians. In 1945 Germany and Japan were defeated. The war brought the development of the **atomic bomb** – a destructive and frightening weapon, which threatened the very existence of humankind.

The legacy of the Second World War

The years after 1945 brought **independence** for those countries in Asia and Africa which had previously been part of the **empires** of the European colonial powers (Britain, France, Belgium and the Netherlands). The declining powers of these European countries made it impossible for them to put down demands for independence from **nationalists** in their old colonies. Within twenty years of the end of the war the old empires had largely disappeared.

Between 1945 and 1948, communist governments were set up in eastern European countries such as Poland and Romania. Most of these countries were now under the control of the USSR. Germany was later split into West and East. West Germany was **democratic** and controlled by Britain, the USA and France. East Germany was communist and controlled by the USSR.

In 1945 the **United Nations** was set up. This was a new peace-keeping body which replaced the Leage of Nations. Despite this, the next 50

"Here you are! Don't lose it again!

A British cartoonist's comment on the importance of the Second World War.

At the stroke of midnight, when the world sleeps, India will awake to life and freedom. It is fitting that at this solemn moment we take the pledge of dedication to the service of India and her people and to the still larger cause of humanity.

Extract from a speech made by Jawaharlal Nehru, the first Prime Minister of India, on the night of 14 August 1947 when India received its independence from Britain.

A cartoon called 'The American voting machine', published in the USSR in 1949. It shows a scene in the United Nations. Behind the US delegate sit politicians from Luxembourg, Holland, Belgium, France and Britain.

years were dominated by the **Cold War**. This was a war of words between the USA (with its allies in western Europe) and the USSR (with its allies in eastern Europe). The western powers were afraid that the USSR wanted to spread communism throughout the world; whereas the east European countries feared that the west would invade them to stamp out communism.

The rivalry was confined largely to a war of accusation and **propaganda**, but there were times when the USA and the USSR came close to direct confrontation. One such occasion was the **Cuban Missile Crisis** of 1962, which could have brought about a Third World War.

In 1989 dramatic changes started to happen. The countries of eastern Europe rejected communism. Democratic governments were set up in Poland, Hungary, Czechoslovakia, Bulgaria and Romania. In 1990, Germany was reunited under a democratic government. Then, in 1991, the communist party in the USSR was abolished. The USSR then broke up into a collection of self-governing countries. The Cold War had ended.

Chaplin

Sir Charles Spencer (1889–1977) was better known to the world as 'Charlie Chaplin'. He was a brilliant comic actor who became famous for his potrayal of a shy, rather sad, baggy-trousered character with a moustache, bowler hat and walking cane. He was one of the great stars of the early silent movie industry.

Chaplin was the son of a British music hall performer and travelled to the United States to pursue his career. In 1914 he made his first film for Keystone Studios. One of his most controversial films, *The Great Dictator*, was made in 1940. In it Chaplin poked fun at the German leader, Adolf Hitler.

2.1 The First World War – Why did it start?

In 1914, the major European countries became involved in a war which was to result in the deaths of over nine million soldiers. It was a war on such a vast scale that people at the time called it the 'Great War', although today we usually refer to it as the First World War.

Why did the countries of Europe want to go to war?

For a war to start countries have to have such strong rivalries that they cannot settle their differences by any other method than fighting. This is what happened in Europe in 1914. By the early years of the 20th century there were two main sets of allies in Europe. Germany, Italy and Austria-Hungary formed the **Triple Alliance**. Britain, France and Russia had joined together in the **Triple Entente**. Each set of allies was highly suspicious of the other and these suspicions were to take Europe into war – especially as the members of each alliance were well armed and powerful.

One of the major rivalries at the time was that between Britain and Germany. Britain was a powerful country with a large Empire which covered a quarter of the globe. To protect its Empire, Britain had the most powerful navy in the world. But the German leader, Kaiser Wilhelm, announced in 1898 that he

A

SOURCE

Private Baldrick: 'I heard that it all started when a bloke called Archie Duke shot an ostrich because he was hungry.'

Captain Blackadder: 'The real reason for the whole thing was that it was just too much trouble not to have a war.'

Extracts from the BBC comedy series 'Blackadder Goes Forth'.

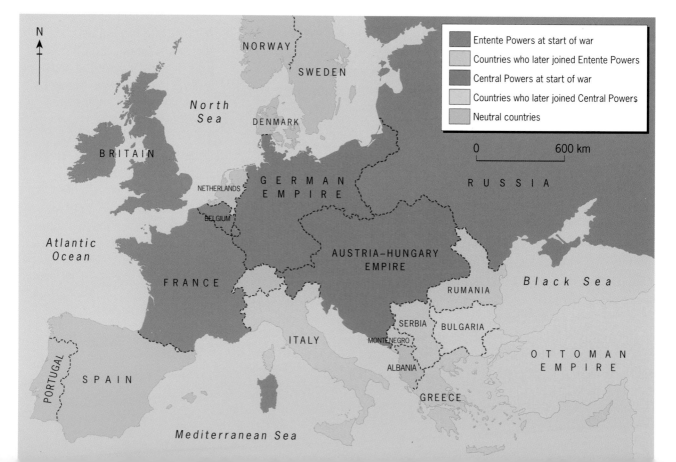

intended to increase the size of Germany's navy. In 1906 Britain launched its first **Dreadnought**, a powerful new battleship. Soon Germany, too, was building Dreadnoughts and a 'naval race' developed between the two countries.

Britain was particularly concerned about Germany because the Germans had already overtaken Britain as an industrial nation. By 1914 Germany was producing more iron, more steel, more coal and even more cars. Kaiser Wilhelm was saying that Germany deserved to have an empire as big as that of France or Britain. Such talk worried Britain and its ally France, since both had large empires which could come under threat.

France had other reasons to oppose Germany. In the Franco–Prussian War (1870–1), the French had suffered a humiliating defeat at the hands of the German state Prussia, and had been forced to hand over the fertile provinces of Alsace and Lorraine. Prussia had then brought the individual German states together to form the new state of Germany. The French wanted revenge for this defeat and they wanted their provinces back.

In eastern Europe two other countries, Austria-Hungary and Russia, were bitter rivals. Both wanted to control the Balkans, an area previously ruled by the Turks. Within the Balkans, Serbia was trying to unite all the Slav people under its rule. Austria-Hungary feared that large numbers of Slavs inside its own borders would want to join Serbia and did all it could to stop the Serbians. Russia, however, was also a Slav country and supported Serbia. Russia thought that a powerful Serbia would be an excellent ally and would make problems for Austria-Hungary.

How did the fighting start?

The event which finally triggered war came on 28 June 1914 in Sarajevo, a town in the Austro-Hungarian province of Bosnia. A Serbian student named Gavrilo Princip assassinated the heir to the Austro-Hungarian throne, Archduke Franz Ferdinand. The Austro-Hungarians accused the Serbian government of helping Princip, and on 28 July invaded Serbia. Russia immediately promised support for its friend and so, on 1 August 1914, Austria-Hungary's ally Germany declared war on Russia. Then, when France began to mobilize its forces to help Russia, Germany declared war on the French as well. Italy decided not to enter the war at this stage. That left just the British. What would their reaction be?

B
SOURCE

An Italian cartoon published just before the outbreak of war. The man shown is Kaiser Wilhelm.

Francis Ferdinand

Francis Ferdinand (1863–1914) was the Archduke of Austria-Hungary. In 1900 he married a Czech princess, Countess Sophie Chotek.

He was heir to the Austrian throne.

He is perhaps best remembered as the victim of the assassination plot which took place on 28 June 1914. As Francis Ferdinand and his wife were on a visit to inspect troops in the Bosnian town of Sarajevo they were shot dead by a Serbian nationalist, Gavrilo Princip.

Following the assassination, Austria-Hungary's declaration of war on Serbia triggered the outbreak of the First World War.

2.2 The First World War – What happened?

The British finally entered the war when the Germans put their **Schlieffen Plan** into operation. This plan involved Germany invading France from the north through Belgium. The Germans believed the French expected the fighting to take place on the Franco-German border, between Metz and Switzerland. If the Germans invaded France from the north, the French would be caught unprepared and soon defeated. Then the Germans could turn their attention to their other enemy, Russia. In the meantime, Austria-Hungary could keep the Russians quiet.

But the German plan failed. Belgium was a neutral country and when Germany invaded, on 3 August 1914, Britain decided to join the war. The British had signed a treaty in 1839 promising to help protect Belgium if it was attacked. So now they declared war on Germany and sent the **British Expeditionary Force (BEF)** to fight the Germans. British intervention could not prevent the huge German army from occupying Belgium, but the BEF did help the French win a victory over the Germans. At the **Battle of the Marne** (5–11 September 1914) the French and British forces (the Allies) finally stopped the advancing Germans after a week of bitter fighting. The Germans retreated 60 kilometres to the river Aisne where they dug deep trenches to protect themselves from enemy fire. To prevent the enemy outflanking them (going around the side of their defences) both sides began to extend their trenches sideways towards the sea and towards the Swiss mountains. By December 1914 the trenches extended nearly 600 kilometres from the Channel coast to the borders of Switzerland.

A For almost a month the Germans had pushed forward, often marching up to 80 kilometres a day. Now they faced an allied counter-attack. The Battle of the Marne was to prove a turning point in history. Under brilliant skies nearly two million men struggled for almost a week along a front over 200 kilometres wide. The French even ferried men from Paris to the battlefield in taxis. By September the Germans had retreated 60 kilometres to the river Aisne. The great advance had been stopped. The German commander, Helmuth von Moltke, told the Kaiser, 'Your Majesty, we have lost the war.'

SOURCE

Nigel Kelly, 'The First World War,' 1989.

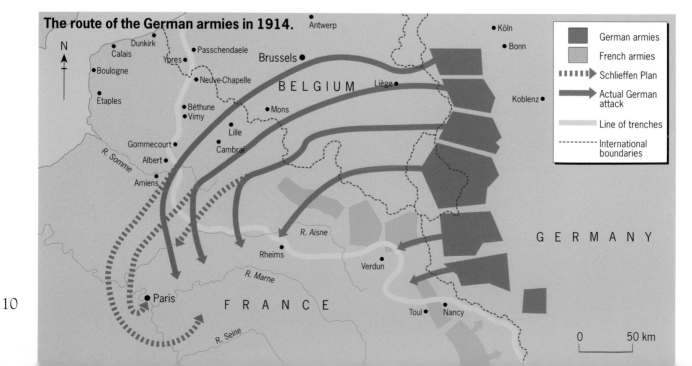

The route of the German armies in 1914.

Legend:
- German armies
- French armies
- Schlieffen Plan
- Actual German attack
- Line of trenches
- International boundaries

0   50 km

Although there was fighting in the First World War from France in the west to the borders of Persia in the east, it was in the trenches of the **Western Front** that the main battles were fought. For the next four years both the Germans and the Allies tried desperately to drive forward and inflict defeat on their enemies. Their attempts to do so cost millions of lives. In 1916 in just two battles, at **The Somme** and **Verdun** the British, French and German forces suffered two million casualties between them. There seemed no way that either side could win the war on the Western Front.

One of the most significant moments in the war came in April 1917 when the **United States of America** joined the war on the side of the Allies. With the injection of fresh troops, it seemed only a matter of time before the Allies ground down the Germans and won the war. But in 1917 the Germans, too, found extra resources when revolution broke out in Russia. This meant that the Russians dropped out of the war. Now the Germans could switch their troops from the Eastern Front to launch a major attack on the Western Front. There was still time to win the war before the flood of new troops arrived from the USA.

So, in March 1918, General Ludendorff began a massive German attack on the Allies. Although they had expected the attack, the Allied forces were pushed back so far by the strength of the German forces that the people of Paris began to prepare to evacuate their city. But the Germans did not have the supplies or reinforcements to sustain their attack. By August the Allies had regained the lost land and the Germans were in retreat. The Germans also had problems at home where the strains of war were becoming too much for the German people. Food supplies were running low and the hungry people were close to rebellion.

When Germany's allies – Bulgaria, Turkey and Austria-Hungary – surrendered to the Allies, Germany's defeat was near. Kaiser Wilhelm was concerned that rioting in Germany might lead to a communist takeover. He therefore agreed to abdicate and leave Germany for Holland. He knew that his absence would make it easier for the German government to surrender and hoped that this would end the riots in Germany. Finally, at 11 am on 11 November 1918, Germany agreed to stop fighting. The war was over.

Haig

Douglas Haig (1851–1928) was born in Edinburgh. He was made Commander-in-Chief of the British forces on the Western Front. He masterminded British military strategy in the trenches and his policy of 'attrition' resulted in appalling casualties during campaigns such as the Somme(1916), and Passchendaele (1917).

After the war, in 1919, Haig was made an earl and set up the 'Poppy Day' appeal to help wounded soldiers.

B

SOURCE

With our backs to the wall and believing in the justice of our cause each man must fight on to the end. The safety of our homes and the freedom of mankind alike depend upon the conduct of each one of us at this critical moment.

Message to the British troops from their Commander-in-Chief, General Haig, in April 1918.

2.3 The Western Front: A Study in Depth

This study will look at what it was like to be a soldier on the Western Front, where most of the major battles of the First World War were fought. It will also consider what those left at home felt about the war, and in what ways attitudes towards the war changed betwen 1914 and 1918.

Why did people volunteer for the Army?

When war broke out in August 1914, Britain did not have an army large enough to fight a major European war. The Prime Minister, Herbert Asquith, therefore asked Lord Kitchener, the War Minister, to take responsibility for raising the necessary number of volunteers to boost the army's numbers. Kitchener issued an appeal in August 1914 for 100,000 men aged between 19 and 35. Soon he was swamped by men desperate to 'do their bit' in the war.

At the outbreak of war neither side expected it to last more than a few months. The Kaiser told his men that they would be 'home before the leaves have fallen from the trees'. In Britain it was widely assumed that it would 'all be over by Christmas'. So there was a great rush to sign up for the army before it was all over. By mid September, half a million men had enlisted and this figure rose to two million by early 1916. Of course, few of the men realized the horrors that lay ahead. For many it was a chance to have fun or see the world. For others it was a chance to escape from dead end jobs and the boring routine of their home lives.

Even for those not keen to join the army there were enormous pressures to sign up. The government carried out a skilful propaganda campaign which portrayed the Germans as evil beasts. It was said that they had bayonetted babies and murdered nuns on their march through Belgium. Recruitment posters emphasized the need to help the country and to protect women and children from the horrors of war. Men who did not join up were made to feel like cowards and women would press white feathers into their hands as a sign of cowardice.

A **SOURCE**

In September 1914 the Northern Foxes Football team of Leeds met to discuss the election of officers and the arranging of fixtures for the 1914–15 season. One of the members suggested that the whole club should enlist, which after some discussion was put to the vote and passed. They joined the Leeds Pals battalion.

M. Brown, 'Tommy Goes to War', 1978.

B **SOURCE**

Perhaps the most famous of all the recruiting posters, Lord Kitchener's appeal for men. By a clever technique wherever you stand this picture seems to be pointing directly at you.

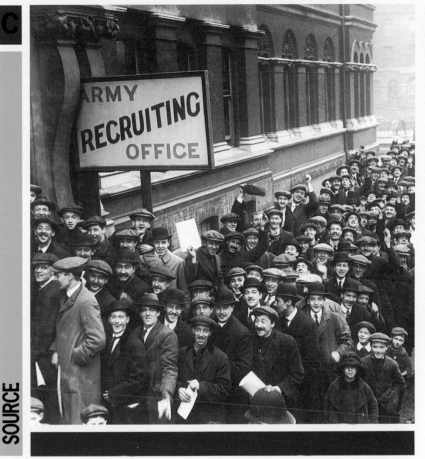

C SOURCE

Smiling recruits outside an army recruiting office in London in 1915.

D SOURCE

I thought it would be the end of the world if I didn't pass. People were being failed for all sorts of reasons: if they hadn't got sufficent teeth, for example. When I came to have my chest measured, I took a deep breath and puffed out my chest as far as I could. The doctor said, 'You've just scraped through.' It was marvellous being accepted. When I got home and told my mother she said I was a fool and she'd give me a good hiding: but I told her, 'I'm a man now, you can't hit a man.'

A *First World War soldier remembers the day he signed up.*

To encourage recruitment the government allowed men from the same area to form their own battalions. This meant that that the recruits were able to serve with their friends and with other men from their local area. These battalions became known as 'pals' battalions and took their names from the city or area in which they were raised. Some cities raised more than one such battalion. There were two 'pals' battalions from Bradford and as many as seven from Manchester. Newcastle even raised a battalion of 'railway pals' from men previously employed in that industry.

Such was the enthusiasm for the war that there were even instances of boys lying about their age to get into the army. In Essex Farm cemetery in Ypres, Belgium there is the grave of the youngest English soldier killed in the war. Valentine Strudwick joined up at the age of 13 years and 11 months. Exactly one year later he was killed by a German shell. His local paper described his death as 'a fine example (and perhaps reproach!) to those of maturer years who have not yet joined.'

Asquith

Henry Herbert Asquith (1852–1928) was the British Prime Minister responsible for declaring war on Germany in 1914.

He became a Liberal MP in 1886 and was Home Secretary in the 1892–5 Liberal Government. In 1905 he was appointed Chancellor of the Exchequer and, in 1908, became Prime Minister.

His government passed several major social reforms. In 1916 Asqiuith resigned to allow Lloyd-George to head the wartime coalition government.

What was it like at the Front?

For most soldiers who joined up the war meant being sent to the Western Front and serving in the trenches. When the two sides 'dug-in' in 1914 they built a complicated system of trenches. The **front line** trenches were designed to protect soldiers from enemy fire. So they were dug two metres deep and almost as wide. They had **sandbags** on top to form a **parapet** as protection against enemy fire. The men walked on **duckboards** to avoid the mud and rested in dug-outs carved into the side of the trenches. When on duty soldiers stood on a **fire-step**, but they had to be careful to keep their heads below the top of the trench – or they would be shot by enemy snipers. Stationed at regular intervals along the trenches were the **machine guns** which could fire 600 bullets a minute at advancing troops. Snipers using rifles with telescopic sights were also positioned along the front line, ready to shoot any enemy soldier foolish enough to raise his head over the parapet.

The trenches

The front line trenches were connected to supplies and reinforcements by a series of **communication, support** and **reserve** trenches. The whole system of trenches might stretch as far as eight kilometres back from the front. The latrines (toilets) for soldiers in the front line trenches were usually just holes cut in the back of the trench. They would have to be moved frequently to stop German snipers from shooting men whilst they were using the toilets.

The trench system.

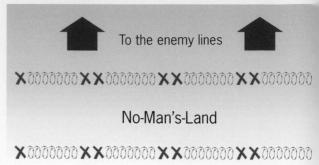

To the enemy lines

No-Man's-Land

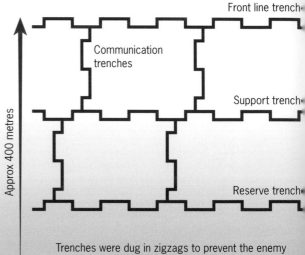

Approx 400 metres

Front line trench

Communication trenches

Support trench

Reserve trench

Trenches were dug in zigzags to prevent the enemy firing along the whole trench if they captured a small part

Cross-section through a front line trench.

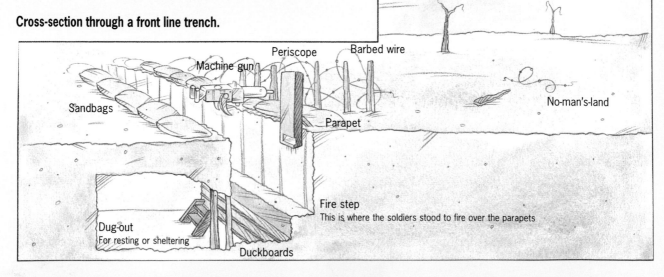

Periscope

Machine gun

Barbed wire

Sandbags

Parapet

No-man's-land

Dug-out
For resting or sheltering

Duckboards

Fire step
This is where the soldiers stood to fire over the parapets

E

F

SOURCE

The battlefield was turned into one huge quagmire, into which were sucked men, horses and guns. It was impossible to get them out once they were in the grip of this terrible mud.

Second Lieutenant James Dale, Liverpool Scottish Regiment describes No-Man's-Land during the Battle of Passchendaele in 1917.

SOURCE

'Hell', a contemporary painting by the French artist Georges Leroux. It shows a First World War battlefield.

In front of the trenches were lines of barbed wire to make it difficult for enemy soldiers to attack. During battles men were often caught up on the barbed wire and many were shot as they lay trapped by the barbs which were as thick as a man's thumb.

Further forward was **No-Man's-Land**. This was the space between the Allied and German trenches. The distance between the trenches varied from two kilometres in some places to less than 50 metres in others. During a battle this area would be so churned up by artillery fire that wounded men sometimes drowned in pools of water that collected in shell

Owen

Wilfred Owen (1893–1918) fought on the Western Front in the First World War. He is, perhaps, the most famous of the 'First World War' poets and his best known work *Dulce et Decorum Est* is a bitter attack on those who supported war. He was killed one week before war ended in 1918.

Everyday life

Daily life for the soldiers depended upon what military operations were taking place in the area. When there was no major battle the troops were supposed to spend four days in the front line, four days in support, four days in reserve and fourteen days resting. But there were instances in battles when men spent over a month in the front line waiting to be relieved.

For front line soldiers the day began with the 'morning hate' when both sides would fire at the enemy for several minutes. Then the men would be divided between those on sentry duty, those responsible for bringing up rations and supplies from behind the lines, and those on trench maintenance. Trenches needed constant repair as a result of damage caused by enemy fire or by poor weather. Men's lives depended on the trenches being secure. An important part of the daily routine was weapon cleaning, to ensure that rifles were free from dirt and rust. A rifle not properly maintained could easily jam and cost a soldier his life. The daily routine was generally very boring for soldiers, but for most it was better to be bored than have to 'go over the top' into No-Man's-Land and face death or injury in an attack on the enemy trenches.

Life was harsh in the trenches; proper sleep was almost impossible and it was common for soldiers to go without a good wash for weeks on end. This led to the men becoming infested with **lice**, which lived in the warm places in a soldier's clothes or on his body. The lice bit the soldiers and made them scratch, often resulting in skin diseases and boils. Lice were very difficult to kill and were best removed by running a candle along the seams of clothes where they tended to congregate.

Private D. J. Sweeney, 1st Battalion of the Lincolnshire Regiment, describes how conditions in the trenches affected him in September 1916.

H SOURCE

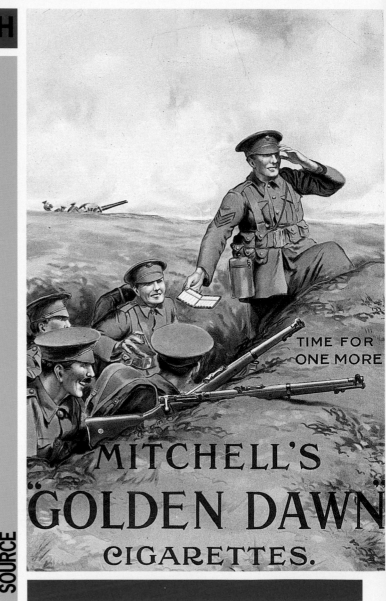

An advertising poster issued in 1915.

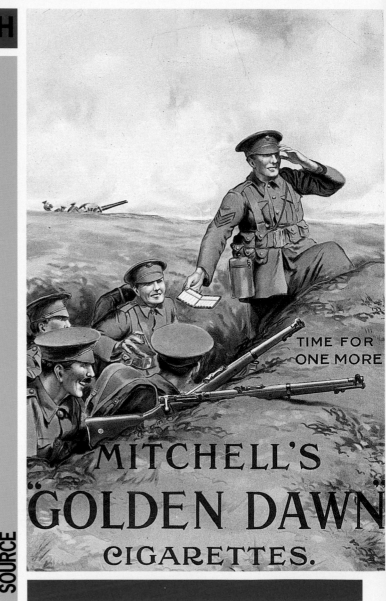
TIME FOR ONE MORE

MITCHELL'S "GOLDEN DAWN" CIGARETTES.

Another problem for soldiers was the enormous numbers of flies. There were thousands of horses at the front and the flies lived on the tons of manure produced by the horses. But the soldiers greatest dislike was reserved for the rats. The soldiers complained that the rats were everywhere. Some of them were described as being 'as big as cats' and gave the men a terrible fright when they woke up in the night to find a rat snuggling down under a blanket with them. The rats also ate any food which was not kept in tins. What the soldiers really hated, however, was the knowledge that the rats grew fat by eating the bodies which lay unburied in No-Man's-Land.

In the cold and wet conditions of winter disease and illness was common. Soldiers contracted dysentery, pneumonia and bronchitis in their thousands. Through constantly having their feet wet many men suffered from a very painful condition called **trenchfoot**. They also suffered from plagues of lice and flies.

Under such difficult conditions it is not surprising that food in the trenches was poor. The main food was tinned bully beef with bread or biscuits. A very popular meal was **Maconochie**, a kind of tinned Irish stew which could be heated quickly over a charcoal brazier. Other treats were bacon, cheese and jam. Proper hot meals were only served when the men were behind the lines and near the field kitchens. In summer a ration of neat lime juice was served. In the winter this was replaced with a tot of rum to help warm the men on a cold day. Drinking water had to be transported from behind the lines and treated with chloride to kill the germs in it. It had an unpleasant taste.

A British soldier who served on the front line in 1915.

Joffre

Joseph Jacques Cesaire Joffre (1852–1931) was a French First World War general. He was responsible for devising French strategy on the Western Front.

He was born in Rivesaltes and entered the army in 1870. By the outbreak of the First World War he had risen to be French Chief of Staff, and, in 1915, was made Commander-in-Chief. He was famous for being a patient and calculating man who played a major part in the implementation of the policy of attrition. However, the heavy casualties suffered by the French army, particularly at Verdun in 1916, led to his replacement.

Trenchfoot, as described by Sergeant Harry Roberts.

What was the fighting like on the Western Front?

The story of the fighting on the Western Front is so sad that some historians have written stinging criticisms of the officers at the front. Even at the time, the politician Winston Churchill, (who as Prime Minister later led Britain in the Second World War) said that the troops were 'fighting machine-gun bullets with the breasts of gallant men'. Others have suggested that the British soldiers were 'lions led by donkeys'.

Generals on the Western Front found it very difficult to devise tactics which could win the war. Many of them were used to wars in which cavalry and infantry charged at the enemy and fought in hand to hand combat. But this tactic did not work in the First World War. The enemy was protected by trenches and had a new weapon to stop enemy attacks. The **machine gun** could fire 600 bullets a minute and cut down advancing enemy forces 'like farmers harvesting corn'. To make a direct attack on the enemy trenches in the face of this weapon was suicide. But this was what the Generals ordered time and time again – they knew of no other way of winning the war. So after the first few months, both sides adopted a policy of **attrition**. This meant that generals planned battles with the idea of wearing the enemy down so that its supply of men and equipment was used up before their own. This policy brought dreadful casualties.

It produces a flooding of the lungs – it is the equivalent to drowning, only on dry land. The effects are these – a splitting headache and terrific thirst [but to drink water is instant death], a knife edge pain in the lungs and the coughing up of a greenish froth off the stomach and the lungs, finally resulting in death.

Lance Sergeant Elmer Cotton describes the effects of chlorine gas in 1915.

Victims of a gas attack.

Weapons

As the war developed both sides tried to find ways round direct attacks on enemy trenches. **Artillery guns** were used to fire shells from behind your own lines into enemy trenches. The guns were designed to destroy enemy defences and protect the infantry as they drove forward. The British used 170 million shells during the war, but often they did no more than churn up the ground in No-Man's-Land and make it harder to cross.

In April 1915 the Germans used a new weapon, **gas**. It had a terrible effect on soldiers. It ate away at their lungs and attacked their eyes so that they went blind. Soldiers who were lightly gassed would probably recover. Others were blinded for life or died a slow and painful death. Soon both sides had gas bombs and carried gas masks as part of their equipment.

In 1916 at the Battle of the Somme, the British introduced a new weapon, the **tank**. The huge rumbling machines terrified the Germans but they were unreliable and most of them broke down. At the Battle of Cambrai in 1917, however, tanks broke through the German trenches and pushed them back nearly eight kilometres. There were still many mechanical problems with tanks, but they proved themselves to be a weapon for the future.

William II

Kaiser William II (1859–1941) was German Emperor and King of Prussia until his abdication in 1918. He was the son of Emperor Frederick and Victoria, the eldest daughter of Britain's Queen Victoria.

He was given a military upbringing and had a great love of military matters. In 1890 he dismissed the statesman, Bismarck, and attempted to assert Germany's claim to world leadership.
When, in November 1918, it became clear that the Allies would not grant Germany peace terms whilst he remained on the throne, he abdicated and went to live in Holland.

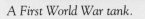

M

SOURCE

A First World War tank.

How severe were the casualties on the Western Front?

Casualties on the Western Front were appalling. Trench warfare brought about death and destruction on a scale previously unknown. The casualty figures for battles on the Western Front in 1916 highlight these terrible losses. In February 1916 the Germans launched a massive attack on the French fortress of Verdun. After months of bitter fighting the German attack was beaten off. The Germans suffered 434,000 casualties in the attack on the French lines and the French lost over 542,000 men fighting off the attack. In July 1916 the British launched a major attack on the Germans along the river Somme. By the end of the year the British had gained 15 kilometres of land and lost 620,000 men. The German casualties were 450,000. In these two battles alone nearly two million men had been killed or wounded.

It has been estimated that during 1918, the British army suffered greater losses than in the whole of the Second World War. Of nearly five million men who joined the British Army during the war one in every five was killed and a further two out of five were wounded. Nearly 500,000 British men were never fit to work again. In total some eight million soldiers died in the war, together with a similar number of civilians.

Number of servicemen killed in the First World War.

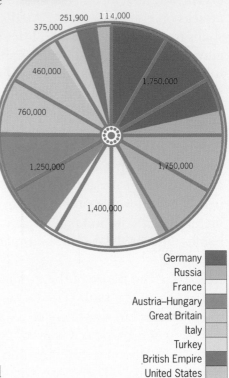

251,900
114,000
375,000
460,000
1,750,000
760,000
1,250,000
1,750,000
1,400,000

Germany
Russia
France
Austria–Hungary
Great Britain
Italy
Turkey
British Empire
United States

A mass burial of war victims.

How did the soldiers react to these losses?

In 1914 men had flocked to join the army. But, as the war ground on, they were less keen to volunteer. Some people felt that thousands of young men were getting out of doing their duty for the country. Therefore, in 1916, the government passed the **Military Service Acts**, which introduced **conscription** – compulsory military service. At first all single men between the ages of 18 and 41 could be called up and, later, married men were also conscripted. Those men undertaking work considered vital to the war effort, such as miners, were exempted from the army.

Some men were **conscientious objectors**. That is, their conscience would not allow them to fight in the war. Such men had to convince a tribunal that they were not just cowards or shirkers. Many men exempted from fighting in this way went to the front and showed great bravery working as stretcher-bearers or doing other support work.

Some conscientious objectors were **absolutists** who refused to have anything whatsoever to do with the war. Between 1914 and 1918 more than 6,000 absolutists were imprisoned and 71 of these died as a result of ill-treatment whilst in prison. In 1918 the government decided that conscientious objectors should lose the right to vote for five years. In the same year a famous philosopher, Bertrand Russell, was imprisoned for six months for publishing a **pacifist** (anti-war) article.

Disillusionment

As casualties at the front mounted, men became increasingly disillusioned with what was happening. In 1917 the French launched an attack which their commander, Nivelle, said would win the war. It failed miserably and cost the French army 117,000 casualties. As a result large numbers of the French army mutinied. More than 23,000 men were found guilty of indiscipline and more than 400 condemned to death (although only 23 were actually shot). Official British army figures show that 3,080 British soldiers were condemned to death during the war and 346 shot by firing squad. Of these, 266 were for desertion, 37 for murder, 18 for cowardice, 7 for quitting position, 6 for striking a superior, 5 for disobedience, 3 for mutiny, 2 for throwing weapons aside and 2 for falling asleep on duty.

SOURCE

We had been brought up to believe that Britain was the best country in the world. We were taught at school that we were better than other people – didn't we always win the last war?. Now we wanted to show the Germans what we could do.

Private George Morgan, 16th Battalion West Yorks Regiment, explains why he signed up in 1914.

Cavell

Edith Louisa Cavell (1865–1915) was an English nurse in the First World War.

She first became interested in nursing during a tour of Europe in 1883 and when she returned home she began training at the London Hospital. She became matron of a hospital in Belgium and was working there when the Germans invaded in 1914. Although she was English her Brussels hospital treated soldiers from both sides in the war.

She also allowed the hospital to be used to hide Allied soldiers escaping from the Germans. When the German authorities discovered this Cavell was arrested in August 1915. Two months later she was executed by firing squad. Her death caused a major outcry in Britain.

P

I continued to go forward until I suddenly became aware that there were few of us in this first line of attack capable of going on. I found myself in the company of Lieutenant Wallace. We dived into a shell hole and began discussing what to do. I came to the conclusion that to go on would be suicidal and that we should stay under cover and pick off any Germans who might expose themselves. Lieutenant Wallace, however, said that we had been ordered to go on at all costs and that we must comply with this order. At this he stood up and within a few seconds dropped down dead riddled with bullets. This left me with the same problem, and having observed his action, I felt that I must do the same. I therefore, stood up and was immediately hit by two bullets and dropped down.

I managed to crawl into a shell-hole into which another colleague of mine had also crawled. He told me that he had been shot through the middle of the back and the bullet had emerged through his left ear. We had not long to wait before a shell burst on the edge of our hole; it killed my colleague and injured me terribly. I considered the situation hopeless and that even if a miracle happened and I did, in fact get away, I would not be fit for anything in this world. I therefore decided to kill myself.

The Medical Officer said that if we were wounded or bleeding we should never drink alcohol as the result would be almost fatal. I had a Worcester Sauce bottle full of rum and I drank it. In fact it just made me slightly merry and bright and caused me to drop off to sleep.

When I came round I came to conclusion that in spite of my condition [my left arm being torn, my left thigh damaged, my right leg wounded and strips of flesh hanging down from my abdomen] it was still worth trying to save myself.

SOURCE

Private Henry Russell recalls his part on the first day of the Battle of the Somme, 1 July 1916.

Q

Towards the end of the war we were so fed up we wouldn't even sing 'God save the King' on church parade. Never mind the bloody King we used to say, he was safe enough; it should have been God save us.

SOURCE

Private J.A. Hooper, 7th Green Howards Regiment.

R

The man in the ranks is no longer aware of why he is fighting.
He has lost both faith and enthusiasm.

SOURCE

Douglas Haig, Commander-in-Chief of British forces, in 1918.

Moltke

Count Helmuth von Moltke (1848–1916) was the German General responsible for putting the Schlieffen Plan into action in 1914.

Moltke became Chief of the German General Staff in 1906. Following Germany's defeat at the Battle of the Marne in 1914 Moltke was blamed for the failure of the German plan and relieved of his post.

How was life for civilians affected by the war?

The First World War had a greater effect on the lives of the civilian population than any previous war. Civilians in Britain soon found that they were under threat from German **bombing**. Zeppelin airships and Gotha bombers carried out raids on Britain which killed nearly 1,400 people and injured 3,300 more. Such raids led to attacks on Germans living in Britain. Also the government put all foreign men of fighting age in camps until the war was over. This was called **internment**. The Royal Family also thought it wise to change its surname from 'Saxe-Coburg-Gotha' to the less German-sounding 'Windsor'.

There were also great restrictions on the British population. **The Defence of the Realm Act (DORA)** of 1914 gave the government wide powers to take over industries, censor newspapers and even order brewers to water down beer. In 1917 **food rationing** began. German submarines were sinking merchant ships laden with food from abroad. Much of the imported food was needed for the troops, so civilians were restricted in what they could buy. Wealthy people, however, were often able to pick up goods in short supply on the **black market** – buying food illegally at higher prices. Conditions were even worse in Germany where there was a flourishing trade in potato peelings and food riots in the winter of 1916.

The war saw an important change in the **position of women** in society. With so many men away, women were needed to work in a variety of jobs from farming to heavy engineering. Before the war some women, the **Suffragettes**, had been carrying out a campaign of violence against the government to win the vote for women. When war broke out the Suffragettes called off their campaign and pledged support for the war effort. Many men were highly impressed with the contribution made by women in the war and were forced to change their old views that women were second-class citizens. After the war in 1918 women were given the vote, although they had to be aged 30 or more. Men could vote at the age of 21.

Astor

Nancy Astor (1879–1964) was born as Nancy Witcher Langhorne in Virginia, USA and married William Wardorf Astor. When her husband became a Viscount in 1919 he had to give up being MP for Plymouth. His wife, Nancy, was elected to take his place as the Conservative MP for Plymouth. She was the first woman to sit in the British House of Commons.

SOURCE

Women munition workers, painted in 1917, by E.F. Skinner. The artist was appointed by the government to paint pictures of the war.

News from the Front

Perhaps the greatest strain for the people at home was the sheer worry of what was happening at the front and not knowing whether a loved one was safe. News of great Allied victories merely added to the fear. No matter how successful an attack might be, there were always casualties – and the constant fear of receiving a telegram with the news that a loved one had been killed. As the number of casualties mounted during the war, hundreds of thousands of such telegrams were sent, resulting in widespread grief throughout the nation.

SOURCE U

I arrived at the cottage that morning to find his mother and sister standing in distress in the midst of his returned kit, which was lying opened all over the floor. The garments sent back included the outfit he had been wearing when he was hit – the tunic torn back and front by the bullet, the khaki vest dark and stiff with blood.

The writer, Vera Brittain, describes how her fiance's relatives received his possessions shortly after he had been killed in France.

SOURCE T

I have been requested to convey to you and to your family an expression of the utmost sympathy with you on the death of your husband… . Your husband died almost instantaneously, while on duty, as the result of a shell bursting in his trench. I must say that his injuries were mostly internal and caused no disfigurement of the features.

Letter from a platoon sergeant to a soldier's widow.

The Bradford Pals battalion suffered heavy casualties during the Battle of the Somme in 1916. The losses were reported week after week in the local press.

SOURCE V

At the end of the war

By November 1918, German troops on the Western Front were on the run. Its allies no longer wished to continue the war and Germany stood alone. At home the German people had reached breaking point and there were riots in the street. There was little choice but to accept defeat and hope for lenient terms from the Allies. So it was that, at 11am on 11 November 1918, the First World War came to an end when the Germans surrendered to the Allies. Yet the killing went on to the bitter end. Even as late as 10.50am on the final day, British troops were killed in an attack on a German held bridge in France. Ten minutes later it was all over.

People were left to mourn the dead and reflect on the great waste of human life. Memorials were built in virtually every village and town to remember those who were killed in the war.

A letter home from a soldier talking about an attack made on the Germans on 6 November 1918.

Scottish Record Office, 'The First World War', 1986.

The war memorial in Chelmsford, taken in the 1920s.

Hindenburg

Paul von Hindenburg (1847–1934) was a German First World War General who later became President of Germany.

Hindenburg was educated in military schools and fought in the Franco-Prussian war of 1870–1. He retired from the army in 1903, but was recalled in 1914 and sent to Russia as Commander-in-Chief on the Eastern Front. Under his command the Germans won two major victories at Tannenberg and Masurian Lakes. After the war Hindenburg was seen as a great military hero and, as a mark of respect, was made President of the new German Weimar Republic, though with very little actual power. In 1932 Hindenburg defeated Adolf Hitler in elections for the Presidency, but in 1933 he was forced to offer Hitler the position of Chancellor.

3.1 The Russian Revolution, 1917–24

a1917 was a dramatic year for Russia. In February the last Tsar, Nicholas II, was overthrown and in a second revolution in October the **Bolsheviks** (later called communists) took over the government. What had caused these dramatic events?

There was widespread discontent with the Tsar's government in the years before the First World War. The Tsar had almost complete control in government. He appointed all ministers and did not have to take advice from anyone unless he wanted to. He used the army and the secret police to control the country. The Tsar was enormously wealthy and lived a luxurious life cut off from the vast majority of Russian people. Yet anyone who dared to criticize the Tsar's rule was liable to be punished either by death or exile to Siberia.

The great majority of Russian people were peasants and factory workers who lived in terrible poverty. There was, however, little that the people could do to improve their lives. Protests or strikes were dealt with harshly by the government.

Many of the educated middle classes in Russia complained about the Tsar's rule. They admired the freedom of speech and lack of censorship that existed in Britain and France and wanted the Tsar to reform Russia to make it more like the west. In 1905 the Tsar agreed to set up a parliament in Russia, but it had little power.

Other opponents of the Tsar followed the ideas of the 19th century German writer, **Karl Marx**, who believed that workers should rise up and take control of their country. The best known of the Marxist groups was the Bolsheviks, who wanted the complete overthrow of the Tsar. Not surprisingly the Tsar's secret police arrested and exiled any Bolsheviks they could catch.

The First World War was a disaster for Russia. The army was defeated on the Eastern Front, and there were food shortages and rising prices at home. People lost faith in the Tsar's ability to govern the country. In February 1917 there were demonstrations and food riots in the city of Petrograd. When soldiers sent to quell the riots refused to fire on the rioters, the Tsar realized that he had lost control and abdicated.

An account of conditions in Russia from B. York, 'The Soviet Union', 1983.

The war had a devastating effect on Russia.

A painting showing the storming of the Winter Palace, the headquarters of the Provisional Government.

A 'Provisional Government' was set up, but when Russia suffered further defeats in the war and food prices continued to rise, it lost control. In Petrograd a **Soviet** (a council of workers, soldiers and peasants) set itself up in opposition to the Provisional Government. When the Bolshevik leader, **Lenin**, promised the people 'Peace, Bread and Land' he won widespread support. In October 1917 Bolshevik soldiers (known as the Red Guard) arrested the leaders of the Provisional Government. Lenin then announced that power had passed to the Petrograd Soviet.

Lenin immediately signed the **Treaty of Brest-Litovsk** to get Russia out of the First World War. Germany agreed to withdraw its forces from Russia, in return for large chunks of Russian territory. Then the Bolsheviks had to fight a bloody civil war against the 'Whites' (anti-Bolshevik forces). The civil war put a terrible strain on the Russian people and there was much opposition to Lenin. By 1921 the 'Whites' had been defeated. The Bolsheviks changed their name to the Communist Party and, in 1923, Russia became the communist **Union of Soviet Socialist Republics (USSR)**.

Marx

Karl Marx was born in Trier in Germany in 1818. He attended universities in Berlin and Bonn where he studied philosophy and history. With another famous philosopher, Friedrich Engels, he wrote the *Communist Manifesto* which encouraged workers to overthrow their rulers.

Marx went to live in London where he wrote his famous book, *Das Kapital*. In this book he wrote that everyone should have an equal share of wealth and power. These views are the basis of modern Communism, which established itself in Russia in 1917. Marx died in England in 1883.

3.2 The League of Nations

The League of Nations was the idea of the President of the USA, **Woodrow Wilson**. The aim of this organization was to encourage the countries of the world to work together. He hoped that they might sort out their problems by discussion (**negotiation**) instead of by fighting. He also hoped that the League could help reduce the numbers of weapons made by the countries of the world.

Wilson hoped that the League would give **collective security** to its members – that is, countries would stand together and protect each other. If a country attacked a member of the League, the other members could stop trading with the attacker. This is known as **applying sanctions**. If this did not work then the League countries could send soldiers to help beat off the attack. The League would also do things such as help **refugees**, and help stop **slavery** and **drug addiction**. After the First World War, the defeated countries lost their empires. Some of these areas were governed by the victorious Allies on behalf of the League. They were called **mandates**.

A **SOURCE**

The League never truly had world support and quickly turned into a talking shop, dominated by countries which won World War I. At times they were able to bully small countries into submission; but they were powerless to influence the other great nations.

B. Catchpole, 'A Map History of the Modern World', 1982.

The structure of the League of Nations.

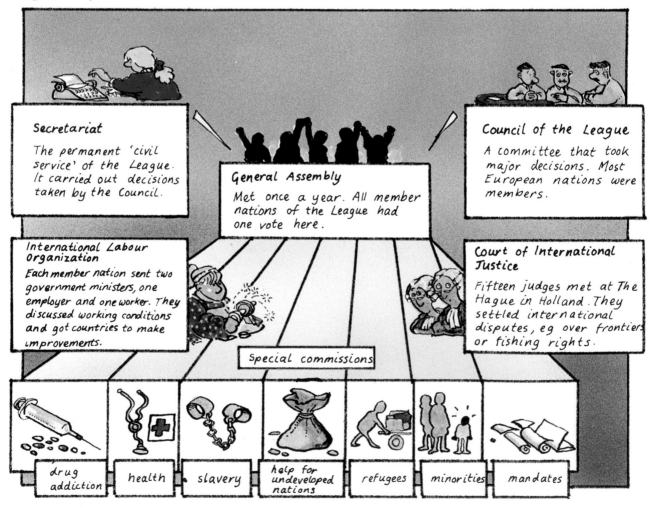

Secretariat

The permanent 'civil service' of the League. It carried out decisions taken by the Council.

General Assembly

Met once a year. All member nations of the League had one vote here.

Council of the League

A committee that took major decisions. Most European nations were members.

International Labour Organization

Each member nation sent two government ministers, one employer and one worker. They discussed working conditions and got countries to make improvements.

Court of International Justice

Fifteen judges met at The Hague in Holland. They settled international disputes, eg over frontiers or fishing rights.

Special commissions

drug addiction | health | slavery | help for undeveloped nations | refugees | minorities | mandates

The League was set up in 1920. Between 50 and 60 countries were eventually members.

In 1921 the **Court of International Justice** was set up by the League in the city of **The Hague**, in the Netherlands. It had fifteen judges from different countries. Governments could bring their disputes to Court and the judges would decide who was right or wrong, and how the dispute could be settled.

The League paid for the **International Labour Organization**. This encouraged governments to provide better wages and working conditions for workers in their country. This did lead to some improvements.

The League had some successes. In 1920 it helped settle a dispute between Sweden and Finland about who should govern the **Aaland Islands** in the Baltic. In the same year the League settled a dispute between Yugoslavia and Albania and divided an area called Upper Silesia which both Germany and Poland thought they should have. In 1925 it helped sort out a disagreement between Bulgaria and Greece over their frontier. It raised money to help Austria which was facing great financial problems after losing the war. In 1932 the League settled a border dispute between Peru and Colombia.

However, the League had many problems. Although President Wilson was in favour of it, he lost power and the USA did not join. This greatly weakened the League. The USSR was not allowed to join until 1934. Germany was finally allowed to join in 1926 but in 1933 Hitler took Germany out of the League. In over 22 years only 32 disputes came before the Court of International Justice. Most governments wanted to settle their disagreements themselves. This meant that the meetings of different ambassadors (the **Conference of Ambassadors**) came to be more important.

In 1919 Poland used force to take the city of **Vilna** from Lithuania. The League protested but the Conference of Ambassadors let the Poles get away with it. In 1923 the Lithuanians used force to seize the German port of **Memel**. The League protested but did not stop them. In 1923 Italy attacked and seized the Greek island of **Corfu**. The Conference of Ambassadors ordered the Greeks to give in to the more powerful Italians. Many countries were not prepared to use force against those who threatened the peace.

Wilson

Woodrow Wilson (1856–1924) was elected President of the USA in 1912. He kept his country out of the First World War until 1917. Towards the end of the war he issued his 'Fourteen Points' as a basis for peace talks. He represented the USA at Versailles where he proposed a 'League of Nations' should be set up. However, he could not persuade the Americans to join. In 1919 he had a stroke and was an invalid until his death in 1924.

3.3 Challenges to Peace

During the 1930s there were a number of challenges to world peace. The failure of the League of Nations to deal with these challenges destroyed its credibility, and therefore made another world war much more likely.

In 1931, the Japanese army invaded **Manchuria**, claiming that the Chinese had damaged the railway at Mukden. The Japanese had soldiers in Manchuria to protect this railway, but the real reason for the invasion was that the army and some members of the Japanese government wanted to capture more land and resources to help solve Japan's economic problems at home.

China appealed to the League of Nations for help. The League sent a team, headed by Lord Lytton, to discover who was to blame. Lytton blamed the Japanese. In 1933, Japan left the League in protest at this but by then had completed the conquest of Manchuria, which it renamed **Manchukuo**. The League was powerless to prevent Japan's success, as its members were not prepared to take military action against Japan. In 1937, the Japanese launched a full-scale invasion of China, and once more China appealed for help. But the leading European powers were not prepared to take action which might harm their fragile economies, and so by 1938 Japan had captured most of eastern China.

A **SOURCE**

The Manchurian affair had three very important results. First, it showed that the League of Nations was not capable of keeping world peace. Second, it encouraged the European dictators to try the same tactics in Africa and Europe. Third, the Japanese had no hesitation about extending their empire by armed force.

B.Catchpole, 'A Map History of the Modern World', 1982.

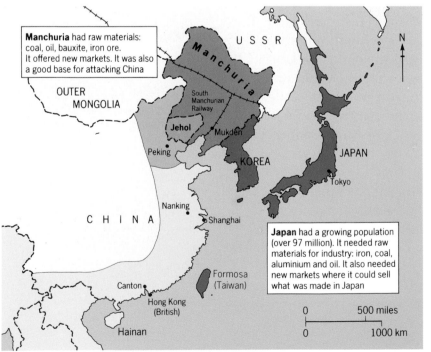

Manchuria had raw materials: coal, oil, bauxite, iron ore. It offered new markets. It was also a good base for attacking China

Japan had a growing population (over 97 million). It needed raw materials for industry: iron, coal, aluminium and oil. It also needed new markets where it could sell what was made in Japan

Japanese expansion in Asia in the 1930s

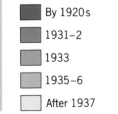

Extent of Japanese occupation
- By 1920s
- 1931–2
- 1933
- 1935–6
- After 1937

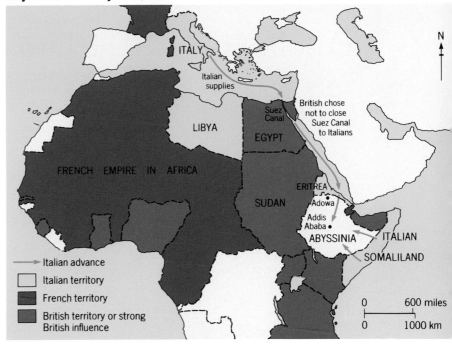

Italy's invasion of Abyssinia, 1935–36

Map labels: ITALY, Italian supplies, LIBYA, Suez Canal, British chose not to close Suez Canal to Italians, EGYPT, FRENCH EMPIRE IN AFRICA, SUDAN, ERITREA, Adowa, Addis Ababa, ABYSSINIA, ITALIAN SOMALILAND, N

Legend:
→ Italian advance
Italian territory
French territory
British territory or strong British influence

0 — 600 miles
0 — 1000 km

In Italy, the Fascist dictator, Mussolini, saw that aggression would not be opposed by the League. He was keen to build a new Roman Empire. Italy already controlled Eritrea and Italian Somaliland in East Africa. In 1935 Mussolini attacked **Abyssinia** (now known as Ethiopia). The Abyssinians had few modern weapons and faced poison gas and aircraft.

Abyssinia appealed to the League for help. Italy was a European country and the major powers took steps to stop the invasion. In October 1935, the League decided to impose **sanctions** on Italy. This meant no longer selling certain goods to them.

However, the British and French were afraid of taking strong action in case Mussolini became an ally of Hitler. So the sanctions did not include the sale of steel, copper or oil. These were just the kinds of things Italy needed to fight a modern war. The League's decision meant that Italy carried on attacking Abyssinia, and by 1936 the Italians had completed the conquest of the country. Mussolini then took Italy out of the League.

The fears of the British and French proved well founded. In 1936, Mussolini and Hitler signed an alliance called the **Rome-Berlin Axis**.

The members of the League had shown that they were not prepared to take the tough action necessary to prevent war. When civil war broke out in Spain in 1936, Hitler and Mussolini helped the Spanish nationalists (led by General Franco) to win the war. The Western democratic countries refused to get involved and the League took no action to end the war. The League had been exposed as weak and without teeth. This did not go unnoticed in Germany where Adolf Hitler was re-building Germany's military might.

B

SOURCE

It is a question of the very existence of the League; of the value of the promise made to small states that their independence shall be respected. God and history will remember your judgement.

The Abyssinian Emperor, Haile Selassie, in a speech to the League of Nations, 1935.

Haile Selassie

Haile Selassie (1892–1975) was born as Ras (Prince) Tafari. In 1930 he became Emperor of Ethiopia but was driven from the country by an Italian invasion in 1935. He was restored to his throne in 1941. He was overthrown again in 1974 by a military coup, which followed years of poverty and starvation. Some Africans (the Rastafarians) still see him as a god.

3.4 Adolf Hitler – The Growing Threat

German crowds cheer soldiers as they enter the Rhineland, 7 March 1936.

B SOURCE

The 48 hours after the march into the Rhineland were the most nerve-racking of my life.

Adolf Hitler, overheard talking to his generals soon after the event.

C SOURCE

The German army was not strong enough for war; its officers had orders to retreat at once if the French began to fight. Hitler need not have worried. Some French generals were secretly fascist. Others were only prepared to defend French territory. They told their government that the French army was not fit to launch an attack.

L.Snellgrove, 'The Modern World Since 1870', 1981.

D SOURCE

France was going through a crisis of leadership and Britain felt Hitler's demands were not entirely unreasonable.

S.Lee, 'Nazi Germany', 1989, on why no action was taken over the Anschluss.

In January 1933 Hitler became the ruler of Germany. Hitler and his Nazi Party were determined to rebuild German military strength and free Germany from the shackles of the hated Treaty of Versailles. In 1933 Hitler withdrew Germany from the League of Nations and secretly began to build a new airforce. He introduced **conscription** (compulsory military service) and began building new tanks, submarines and ships. These measures went against the Treaty of Versailles. However, there were many in Britain, in particular, who thought that Germany had been harshly treated at Versailles. So there was little opposition to his measures.

In 1935 the Saar voted to return to Germany – it had been under the control of the League since 1919. This showed how popular Hitler was in Germany and gave him back the coal and iron and steel works that were in this area.

In 1935 France, Britain and Italy agreed to form the **Stresa Front**, to stand together against Germany. Soon Britain broke this agreement and signed the **Anglo-German Naval Treaty**, which allowed a larger German navy. Then Italy fell out with France and Britain over their reaction to the attack on Abyssinia. The agreement was in ruins.

In March 1936 German troops re-entered the Rhineland. The keeping of German troops in this area was forbidden by the Treaty of Versailles. The British and French protested but refused to act. Many argued that the Rhineland was German territory and Hitler could do what he liked with it. Hitler decided the democracies of Europe would be unwilling to stop him if he made other attempts to make Germany more powerful. That same year he formed an alliance with Italy, called the **Rome-Berlin Axis**.

The Treaty of Versailles banned Germany and Austria from being united but Hitler was determined to bring all the German speaking people together in one country. Pressure was put on the Austrian government and its leader, **Von Schuschnigg**, was invited to Germany. Here he was threatened and forced to make the Austrian Nazi Party legal and release Nazi terrorists who were in prison. On his return to Austria, Von Schuschnigg decided to let the Austrian people decide. He ordered a vote, called a **plebiscite**. Hitler was furious. He ordered Austrian Nazis to revolt and called on Mussolini for support. Von Schuschnigg was forced to resign and was replaced by a Nazi. On 12 March 1938, German troops crossed the frontier and united the two countries (the *Anschluss*). This was the first time Hitler had defied the Treaty of Versailles outside Germany. Once again Britain and France took no action.

Hitler

Adolf Hitler (1889–1945) was born in Branau in Austria. He left school at the age of 16 with few qualifications. He joined the Germany army in 1914. He fought with distinction in the First World War and won the Iron Cross.

In 1921 he became leader of the German Workers' Party (later called Nazi Party) and, from January 1933, was Chancellor of Germany. He established a totalitarian regime in Germany. In 1939 he took Germany into war with Britain and France. As defeat loomed he committed suicide in April 1945.

German troops in Vienna, 1938.

E
SOURCE

3.5 Peace at Any Price?

In the 1930s the western democracies of Britain and France adopted a **policy of appeasement** towards Hitler and Mussolini. This means that they tried to negotiate and meet many of the demands of the dictators in order to avoid war. The Treaty of Versailles had set up the country of **Czechoslovakia** in eastern Europe. Two and a half million Germans lived in the western part of this country, in an area called the **Sudetenland**. After the Anschluss with Austria, German territory surrounded much of western Czechoslovakia. Hitler threatened that if the Sudeten Germans were not given the right to rule themselves (**self determination**) he would declare war on Czechoslovakia.

The British Prime Minister **Chamberlain** flew to Germany on 15 September 1938 to try to persuade Hitler not to fight. Hitler agreed to give the Czechs until 1 October to do as he demanded. Chamberlain put pressure on the Czech leader **Benes** to agree to give up those parts of the Sudetenland in which Germans made up the majority of the population. On 23 September Chamberlain met Hitler once more. The German leader refused to accept what Benes had offered. Instead he demanded that the Czechs give up *all* of the Sudetenland to Germany.

It looked as if war would follow. The Czechs were allies of the French and the USSR, and they had a well-organized small army. On 28 September Chamberlain was invited to meet with Hitler, Mussolini and the French leader Daladier in Munich, Germany. They would try to sort out the problem. The Czechs were not allowed to take part and the USSR was not invited. At this meeting it was agreed that Hitler could have all of the Sudetenland. The Czechs would have to accept the arrangement or fight Germany on their own. Hitler promised he would make no more demands in Europe. On 1 October Germany took the Sudetenland. That month Germany allowed Hungary and Poland to take land from the Czechs, too.

A SOURCE

In war there are no winners but all are losers. It is these thoughts that made me feel it my duty to avoid a repeat of the Great War.

Chamberlain, September 26, 1938.

B SOURCE

I must confess to a distrust of the USSR. I have no belief in her ability to fight. And I distrust her motives.

Chamberlain, April 1939.

C SOURCE

To go into battle without our Empire behind us – and we won't have it on this issue – is unthinkable.

Henderson, British Ambassador to Berlin, September 1938.

D SOURCE

We must reduce the numbers of our potential enemies and gain the support of potential allies.

British military chiefs, 1937.

E SOURCE

In 1938 Britain and France let Hitler have whatever they considered necessary for the peace of Europe. They felt that Hitler had certain definite aims and that once he had achieved these he would be satisfied.

S. Lee, 'Nazi Germany', 1989.

How Czechoslovakia was divided, 1938.
Given to Germany at Munich
Seized by Poland, September
Given to Hungary by Germany and Italy, October
N
GERMANY
Sudeten Germans
Silesia
POLAND
Prague
Kracow
CZECHOSLOVAKIA
Teschen
Brno
miles
0
100
0
200
km
Danube
Vienna
Bratislava
AUSTRIA
HUNGARY
ROMANIA
Budapest

F Chamberlain decided that the demand for the return of the Sudetenland was reasonable. Here was another Versailles mistake which needed correcting.

L. Snellgrove, 'The Modern World Since 1870', 1968.

G It was a deliberate policy aimed at directing the violence eastward and against the USSR.

A later Soviet view of appeasement. From 'Recalling the Past', published by the Novosti Press Agency, Moscow, 1985.

Nothing to do with Britain
British Empire won't help
Germans treated badly after WWI
Britain had too many possible enemies
?
Hitler would soon stop making demands
British army not ready for war
Fear of Communist USSR
Fear of war

Why did Chamberlain adopt a policy of appeasement?

Chamberlain

Neville Chamberlain (1869–1940) is famous as the British Prime Minister of the 1930s who tried to avoid war.

Chamberlain's Public Offices

1905	Lord Mayor of Birmingham
1918	MP for Birmingham
1923	Minister of Health
1931	Chancellor of the Exchequer
1937	Prime Minister

Chamberlain believed that direct, one-to-one discussions with Hitler could avoid war. This policy was bitterly opposed by Winston Churchill, who believed that Chamberlain should take a more confrontational approach. Although Chamberlain reached agreement with Hitler at Munich in 1938, Hitler broke his promises. Chamberlain abandoned his policy of appeasement in 1939. After the invasion of Norway, Chamberlain resigned.

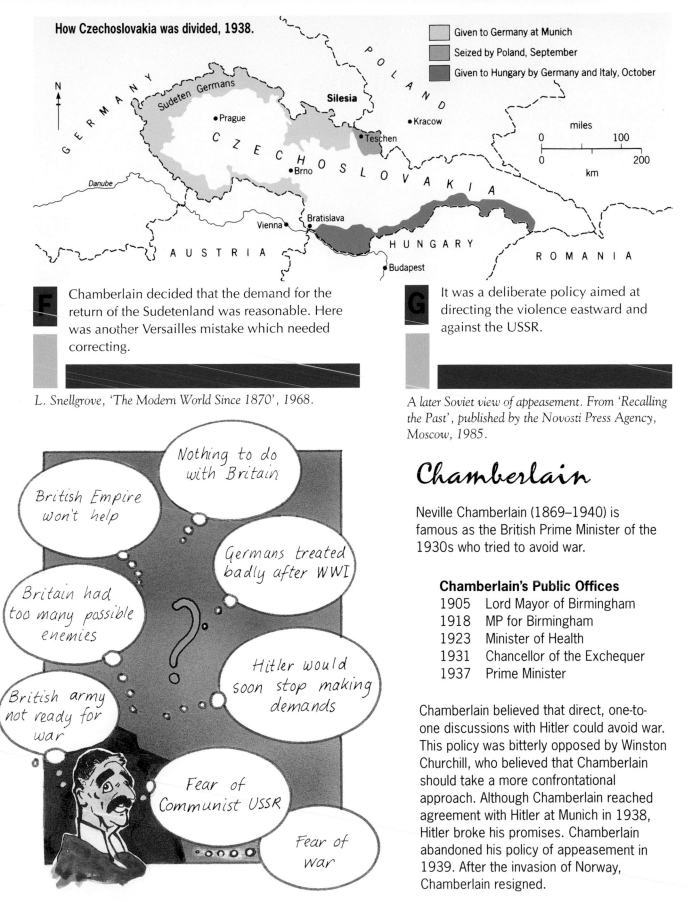

3.6 1939: The Collapse of Peace

In 1939 the peace in Europe was shattered and the Second World War began. The policy of appeasement had failed. Hitler had finally pushed the western democracies too far.

On 15 March 1939 Hitler broke his promise to the Czechs and seized the western parts of the country, called **Bohemia** and **Moravia**. Only the eastern part, called **Slovakia**, was left and it was a puppet state of the Germans. Hitler also allowed his friends the Hungarians to take a chunk of eastern Slovakia, called **Ruthenia**.

One week later Hitler seized the city of **Memel** from **Lithuania**, on the Polish borders. The British were shocked and promised that they would stand by the Poles if Germany attacked. The Germans wished to control the **'Polish Corridor'** which divided the bulk of Germany from the Germans of East Prussia and which gave Poland a route to the sea. Already Nazis were active in the city of **Danzig** (modern **Gdansk**) which was run by the League of Nations.

A SOURCE

The final steps to war, 1939.

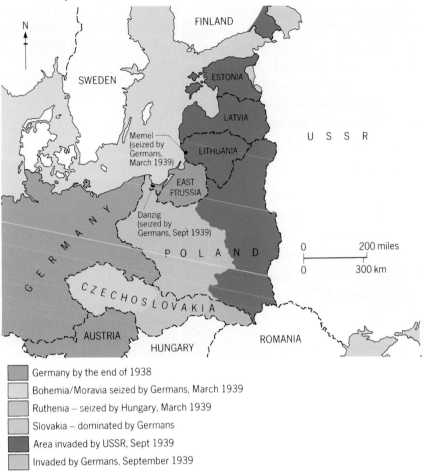

- Germany by the end of 1938
- Bohemia/Moravia seized by Germans, March 1939
- Ruthenia – seized by Hungary, March 1939
- Slovakia – dominated by Germans
- Area invaded by USSR, Sept 1939
- Invaded by Germans, September 1939

From a Polish newspaper, August 1939.

The Soviet leader Stalin in July 1941, justifying his alliance with Hitler in 1939.

Molotov

Vyacheslav Molotov was a Soviet statesman who played an important role in relations between the USSR and the West between 1939 and 1956. He took part in the Bolshevik Revolution and was appointed to the Politbureau (inner council) in 1921. He became Chairman of the Council of Ministers in 1930 and Foreign Minister in 1939. He was largely responsible for the negotiations which brought about the Nazi-Soviet pact of 1939. During the war he advised Stalin on foreign policy, but his influence declined after Krushchev took power. He was ambassador to Mongolia from 1957 to 1960 and then retired from public life.

In April 1939 the Italians invaded **Albania**. The British then promised **Greece** and **Romania** that they would stand by them if they were attacked. The British leaders no longer trusted Hitler and his allies. They hoped that by finally standing up to him a war could still be avoided. On 18 April the USSR asked Britain and France to make an agreement that they would defend each other if attacked. The British leaders did not like the Communists and did not reply with any enthusiasm or speed.

Then the seemingly impossible happened. On 23 August Germany and the USSR signed an agreement promising not to attack one another. This was called the **Nazi–Soviet Pact**. A secret part of the pact was an agreement to share Poland's lands between the two countries. On 1 September Germany invaded Poland. On 3 September Britain and France declared war. They believed that this was the only way to stop the spread of German power.

How did the Nazis win power in Germany?

Hitler's time in prison convinced him that he could not win power by staging a revolution; instead he had to win the support of the people. After the war the Weimar Republic (as the government of Germany was now called) faced many problems. In 1924 **Gustav Stresemann** became Chancellor (Prime Minister). He overcame many of the Republic's problems and restored Germany's relations with the other European powers. For a while, Germany seemed to be doing well and so people felt little need to join Hitler's new party.

Hitler, therefore, had to wait until the time was right. He re-organized the party and put **Joseph Goebbels** in charge of propaganda. By 1928, the Nazi Party had more than 100,000 members, but in the elections to the **Reichstag** (Parliament) in May of that year it won only 12 seats.

In 1929 the USA suffered a catastrophic economic slump which brought an end to its prosperity and led to widespread unemployment, poverty and homelessness. During the 1920s the USA had lent huge sums to other countries to help build up their economies. One of these countries was Germany.

Now the Americans wanted their money back. This led to German businesses going bankrupt, or having to produce fewer goods. As a result fewer workers were employed and there were fewer people buying goods – so businesses had to cut back again. Then the cycle was repeated once more! Soon unemployment had soared and the prosperous 'Stresemann era' was over.

Stresemann died early in 1929 and the people who succeeded him could not cope with the terrible problems that Germany now faced. In desperation the German people turned to the extreme ideas of the Nazis and communists. There were three elections in the period 1930–32 and in each support for these two parties increased. In April 1932 Hitler stood against **President Hindenburg** in the elections for the post of President. He lost but still won the votes of 13.5 million Germans. Then, in the Reichstag elections of July 1932, the Nazi party won 230 seats – almost 100 more than the next largest party. In elections later in the year they again won more seats than any other party. So, in January 1933, President Hindenburg invited Hitler to become Chancellor.

D SOURCE

Year	Number of People Unemployed
1928	1 862 000
1929	2 850 000
1930	3 217 000
1931	4 886 000
1932	6 042 000

Unemployment in Germany 1928–32.

E SOURCE

Year	Nazis	Communists
1928	12	54
1930	107	77
1932 (July)	230	89
1932 (Nov)	196	100
1933	288	81

Seats won by the Nazis and Communists in the Reichstag elections, 1928–33.

F SOURCE

The assembly hall was decorated with swastikas and Hitler uttered dark threats about what would happen if we did not vote for the Enabling Law. The SA and SS people, who surrounded us in a semi-circle along the walls of the hall, hissed loudly and murmered 'Shut up', 'Traitors', 'You'll be strung up today'.

A member of a party in opposition to the Nazis describes the scene on the day that the Enabling Law was passed.

The Reichstag on fire, 27 February 1933.

The Enabling Law 1933

At this point Hitler did not yet have a majority of seats in the Reichstag. So he called a new election for March 1933, and set about trying to win a majority. During the election campaign, he stepped up propaganda praising the Nazis and drafted 50,000 Stormtroopers and **SS** members (a new organization of elite soldiers) into the police force to break up meetings of political opponents. Then, on 27 February 1933, the Reichstag building was burned down and a Dutch communist confessed to starting the fire. Hitler was able to persuade President Hindenburg that there was a communist plot against his government. He was granted emergency powers which took away freedom of speech and freedom of the press. Many historians think the Nazis started the fire themselves.

These powers helped the Nazis win more seats at the March election, but they still did not have a majority in the Reichstag. It was only because he had the support of the Nationalist party that Hitler could be sure of getting his way. Hitler decided to introduce an **Enabling Law** which would allow him to rule with complete authority. He would not have to refer to the Reichstag. This change needed a two-thirds majority. Hitler achieved this in two ways. First, he struck a deal with the Centre Party to win its support and then he expelled the communist members from the Reichstag. Second, he surrounded the building where the Reichstag met with Stormtroopers and members of the SS. Not surprisingly many MPs were too frightened to vote against Hitler's proposals and on, 23 March 1933, the Enabling Law was passed by 441 votes to 94. Hitler now had absolute power.

Hess

Rudolf Hess (1894–1987) was Hitler`s deputy Fuhrer during the 1930s. He fought in the First World War and joined the Nazi Party in 1920. He took part in the ill-fated Munich Putsch of 1923 and was imprisoned with Hitler in Landsberg Castle. Here he wrote down the first part of *Mein Kampf* from Hitler`s dictation. In 1941 Hess flew to Britain on a strange peace mission. He was captured and imprisoned for the remainder of the war. At the Nuremburg trials in 1946 he was sentenced to life imprisonment. He remained in Spandau prison in Berlin until his death in 1987.

Why did the German people support the Nazis?

In 1928 the Nazis won only 3% of seats in the Reichstag, but just four years later they were easily the largest party. A major reason for the growth of support for the Nazi Party was discontent with the Weimar Republic. Many people blamed it for Germany's humiliation at Versailles. In 1923 there had been further humiliation when France occupied the Ruhr, Germany's industrial heartland, because Germany had not kept up its reparation payments. This led to a period of hyper-inflation, when the government kept printing more and more money. Eventually, the value of money was reduced to the level where schoolchildren made kites out of bank notes! Gustav Stresemann seemed to have restored the economy, but then came the economic slump of 1929. Many Germans doubted the ability of the Weimar Republic to deal with this latest crisis. They wanted decisive action to produce stability and an end to the cycle of economic disasters.

Not surprisingly, therefore, the Nazis won a great deal of support from the middle classes of Germany, such as teachers, shopkeepers and lawyers. These people were particularly hard hit by Germany's economic problems. Inflation meant their savings were worthless. They believed that strong government was necessary to solve those economic problems.

Many of the working classes were suspicious of the Nazis and gave their support to the Communist Party. However, the high levels of unemployment resulting from the events of 1929 won

H

SOURCE

Children playing with German banknotes in November 1923. Hyper-inflation meant that money had become worthless.

A Nazi Party poster from 1932. The slogan says, 'Our last hope – Hitler'.

J

There were many, however, amongst one's friends and acquaintances who were were ready to give their support to the new government ... 'He's our last chance', I heard all over and over again. 'We've got to let him have this opportunity. After all the Nazis are only a minority in government ... and if the worse comes to the worst, the Army can turn the Nazis out.'

SOURCE

Account from an Englishman living in Germany in the early 1930s.

the Nazis many votes from working-class Germans, who hoped that they would find jobs under a Nazi government.

Big business and industrial leaders were also suspicious of Hitler, but they too saw advantages in supporting the Nazis. Hitler promised law and order and was strongly anti-communist. Here was a party, they thought, under which business could thrive.

Hitler's message also appealed to many other Germans. Ex-soldiers were pleased to hear that they hadn't lost the war, but had been 'betrayed by Jews and communists'. Countless others were attracted by the promise to tear up the hated Treaty of Versailles and restore German military might. It seemed that a vote for the Nazis would mean Germany getting back the pride which it had lost after the war. Hitler's propaganda reinforced this message and his Stormtroopers continued to threaten political opponents. So support for the Nazis grew.

Owens

John Cleveland Owens (1913–80) was better known as 'Jesse' Owens. In an athletics meeting in 1935 he broke six world records in just 45 minutes!

In 1936 Owens took part in the Olympic Games in Berlin and became the only man to win four track and field gold medals in a single Olympics. His success angered Hitler.

How did the Nazis stay in power 1933–39?

In March 1933 Hitler had established himself as absolute ruler in Germany. He now set about making sure that the Nazis would stay in power. This he did by crushing any opposition, by skilfully using propaganda, and by carrying out policies which were popular with the German people.

The crushing of opposition

In July 1933, using the powers granted to him by the Enabling Act, Hitler banned all political parties except the Nazis. In 1934, when President Hindenburg died, Hitler combined the offices of President and Chancellor under one title – Führer. From now on members of the army swore a personal oath of allegiance not to Germany, but to 'Adolf Hitler, Führer of the Reich'.

Hitler knew that the army generals did not approve of his private army, the Stormtroopers. He needed the support of the army to stay in power so, on 30 June 1934, he ordered the SS to execute Ernst Röhm and over 70 other SA leaders. This was known as the **Night of the Long Knives.** The SA was broken and from now on had little influence.

Hitler was quite prepared to use terror tactics to maintain control. Most Germans never came into conflict with the Nazi regime, but those who dared to oppose it were dealt with in a ruthless manner. The **Gestapo** (secret police), set up in 1933, was told to discover the enemies of the state and make them harmless. It was assisted in its work by the SS.

A cartoon from the 'Evening Standard' of 3 July 1934. Hitler is holding the gun, Goering is carrying a spear and Goebbels is on his knees behind Hitler.

K

The Führer has been shown the enclosed press cutting concerning the sentencing of the Jew, Markus Luftgas, to two and a half years imprisonment. The Führer desires that Luftgas should be sentenced to death. I would be obliged if you would make the necessary arrangements as soon as possible.

A letter issued by one of Hitler's staff to a provincial governor.

L

By 1939 the Gestapo had arrested and taken into 'protective custody' 162, 734 opponents of the Nazi regime. In addition, there were 21,000 prisoners in concentration camps run by the SS. Between 1934 and 1939, 534 Germans were executed for 'political offences'. Since judges were appointed only if they supported the Nazis, those who were arrested could expect little justice in the courts.

Nazi control was even carried into the workplace. Trade unions were banned and many of their leaders imprisoned. The Nazis set up their own trade union, the **German Labour Front**. Under the Nazis working hours generally increased by several hours a week, but there was only a small increase in wages.

The Protestant and Catholic Churches were a possible source of opposition to the Nazis and at first Hitler tried hard to remain on good terms with both of them. In 1933 he signed an agreement (the Concordat) with the Catholic Church. Hitler promised not to interfere in church matters if the Catholic Church kept out of politics. But, support from the churches turned to opposition as Hitler's policies of political oppression and anti-semitism increased. He also tried to extend his control over the churches and shut down Catholic Youth movements as they rivalled his own Hitler Youth. In 1937 the Pope denounced Nazism as anti-Christian. Hitler replied by sending nuns and priests to labour camps. There they were joined by some 800 Protestant ministers, such as **Pastor Niemoller**, who spoke out against the Nazi regime.

The aim of the Labour Front is to educate all Germans who are at work to support the Nazi Party and to train them in Nazi ways.

Proclamation to German workers in 1933.

A Nazi propaganda poster showing Hitler as the saviour of Germany.

Getting the Nazi message across

Hitler was determined that the German people should live their lives according to Nazi beliefs. It was important, therefore, that the correct messages were broadcast to the nation.

In March 1933, Joseph Goebbels was appointed **Minister of Popular Enlightenment and Propaganda**. He soon took control of the mass media in Germany. A law of October 1933 forbade any newspaper from criticizing the government. Goebbels kept a careful eye on what was written in the papers. The Nazis made sure they controlled the radio. Mass production meant that by 1942, seven out of every ten households in Germany owned a radio and so it was important that radio broadcasts portrayed a positive view of Nazism. Control of the press and radio was backed up with extensive poster campaigns portraying Hitler as a great leader and condemning his opponents. Government control was extended to music, books, paintings and films. It was not only political opposition which the Nazis were trying to stamp out. The Jews were particular targets of Nazi propaganda as Hitler drove home his message that they were an inferior race responsible for many of Germany's problems (see Unit 4.8). Certain types of music and art were also judged unsuitable because they were considered 'degenerate'.

The Nazis went to great lengths to ensure that the children were brought up with the correct views. History was re-written to emphasize the part played by the Nazis in Germany's history and subjects such as 'Race Study' appeared on the timetable. Outside school there was an elaborate system of youth movements to reinforce the Nazi message. Boys joined the **German Young People** at 10 and then between 14 and 18 were trained for military service in the **Hitler Youth**. Girls were expected to be members of the **Young Maidens** until they were 14 and then join the **League of German Maidens** until they were 21.

SOURCE

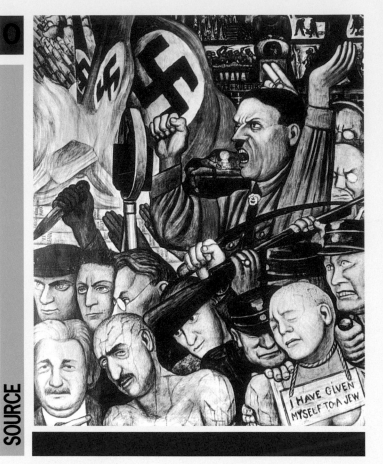

O

A painting by the Mexican artist, Diego Rivera, in 1933. It shows Hitler as a ruler obsessed with violence and brutality. Such a painting would not have been allowed in Germany.

P

SOURCE

In the next issue there must be a lead article, featured as prominently as possible, in which the decision of the Führer, no matter what it will be, will be discussed as the only correct one for Germany.

Instructions issued to the press by the Ministry of Propaganda two days before the outbreak of the Second World War.

Hinaus mit allen Störenfrieden!

Einheit der Jugend in der Hitlerjugend!

A Nazi poster from 1933, encouraging young people to join the Hitler Youth Movement.

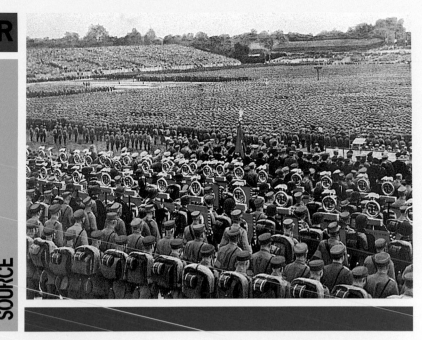

A Nazi Party rally in the 1930s.

A Nazi poster showing the ideal family of four children.

The Nazis had strong views on the role of women in society. They believed that women should remain at home and raise children. To encourage women to have families, contraception was discouraged and mothers with large numbers of children were given a special medal, the Motherhood Cross. In some cities women were banned from smoking in restaurants because it was thought to be unattractive. They were also discouraged from using make up and wearing the latest fashions. Simple peasant styles, with plaited hair and flat heels were encouraged.

The Nazis appreciated how much spectacle could influence peoples' opinions. They therefore held huge rallies with thousands of soldiers marching together. These rallies, often by torchlight, gave Germans a pride in their armed forces and showed how powerful and glorious the country could be. In 1936 the **Olympic Games** were held in Berlin. This gave Hitler a chance to show off his regime, but the games were a disappointment for him. The star athlete was not an Aryan, but a black American, Jesse Owens.

Carrying out popular policies

In 1932 the Nazis had won enormous support in the Reichstag by promising to take steps to solve Germany's economic problems and to create jobs. Unemployment was reduced by a variety of methods. Men were conscripted into the army which increased in size from 100,000 to 900,000 in the 1930s. The Nazis also set up the **National Labour Service** which employed hundreds of thousands of Germans in public works schemes such as building autobahns (motorways), schools and railways. Large sums were also spent on rearming Germany's military forces, thus creating jobs in the armaments industry. Unemployment dropped from six million in 1933 to only 500,000 in 1938. Workers lost many of their rights under the Nazis, but they did at least have jobs.

To make up for the loss of workers' rights the Nazis set up the **Beauty of Labour Organization** which aimed to improve working conditions and encouraged workers to see hard work as a noble and beautiful thing. They also set up **Strength through Joy** which provided leisure activities such as films and holidays for workers who produced lots of goods.

But it was not just the creation of jobs which brought support for the Nazis. In 1933 Germany had been in turmoil and some people feared that a communist revolution might take place. The Nazis had destroyed communism and brought stability. Hitler had built up the German army and was beginning to reclaim the land lost at Versailles (see Unit 2.4). Under strong leadership Germany was getting back its pride. Nazi propaganda even provided someone to blame for the years of difficulty. It wasn't the fault of the

SOURCE

5 Mark die Woche musst Du sparen- willst Du im eignen Wagen fahren!

KdF-Wagen: Über Anschaffungspreis und Zahlungsweise erteilen Auskunft alle Betriebswarte und Dienststellen der NS.-Gemeinschaft „Kraft durch Freude" Gau München-Oberbayern

A poster of 1938 encouraging German workers to 'Save five marks a week and get your own car'. The Volkswagen ('people's car') was introduced by the Nazis.

U

SOURCE

The building of autobahns helped other industries. The workers who built them spent their wages in shops, cafes and on factory goods. The roads also helped the German motor industry, which was the great success story of the 1930s, employing 1.5 million people. This, in turn, helped the growth of the electrical industries.

Norman Stone, 'Hitler', 1980.

German people, it was the Jews, the communists and the Weimar Republic who had caused the problems. Under such circumstances it was not surprising that so many Germans considered that the benefits of Nazi rule outweighed the disadvantages.

Postscript

Hitler stayed in power until 1945. As the Allied powers closed in on Berlin, Hitler committed suicide on 30 April. On 7 May 1945, Germany surrendered. Nazi rule was at an end.

Whatever one thinks of Hitler's methods ... there can be no doubt that he has achieved a marvellous transformation in the spirit of the people ... and in their social and economic outlook. The old trust him, the young idolize him. It is not the admiration accorded to a popular leader. It is the worship of a national hero who saved his country from despondency and degradation...

Extract from an article by David Lloyd George, former British Prime Minister. It was written in the 'Daily Express' in 1936 after Lloyd George had spent three weeks in Germany.

A Strength through Joy poster from the 1930s. It is promising workers homes on new housing estates.

Frank

Anne Frank (1929–45) was German Jew. In 1933, she fled with her family to Amsterdam in Holland to escape the persecution of Hitler's Nazis.

When the Germans invaded Holland in 1941 the Frank family once more found themselves in danger. From July 1942 they were hidden by friends in a sealed office back-room in an Amsterdam warehouse. Then, in August 1944, they were betrayed. The whole family was sent to concentration camps and Anne, her sister and her mother died there. During their time in hiding Anne kept a diary recording details of the family`s life. After the war her father arranged for Anne`s diary to be published and soon she became a symbol of the suffering endured under the Nazis. Anne wrote, 'I want to go on living, even after my death.' Her diary has allowed this to happen.

4.1 War in Western Europe, 1939–41

On 1 September 1939 German troops moved into Poland. They used a new kind of warfare called **Blitzkrieg** (lightning war). First the enemy was 'softened up' by the German **Panzer** tank units and the *Luftwaffe* bombers, then the infantry moved in to mop up. Britain and France both declared war on Germany but could not offer any help to Poland. Stalin also invaded Poland from the east, as had been agreed in the Nazi–Soviet Pact. The Poles were defeated within four weeks.

The British expected Hitler's bombers at any moment. The government tried to prepare for this: gas masks were issued to all civilians; a system of air-raid warnings was set up; lights were blacked out; children from big cities were evacuated to the countryside; cinemas and theatres closed. But for months nothing happened. The lack of fighting led people to nickname this period the 'Phoney War', or more humorously 'Sitzkrieg'!

But in April 1940 war arrived in western Europe. Hitler's forces captured **Norway** and **Denmark**, despite attempts by the British and French to stop them. In May, Chamberlain resigned as Prime Minister and was replaced by **Winston Churchill**. A few days later Hitler launched his attack on France ('**Operation Yellow**'). Germany invaded the Netherlands, Belgium and Luxembourg, then marched on into France, avoiding the **Maginot line**, France's great line of fortifications along the German border. By 20 May German forces had reached the Channel coast.

'Operation Yellow' – the German invasion of France, May 1940.

A SOURCE

A contemporary painting by Charles Cundall showing troops being rescued from the beaches of Dunkirk.

Date	Figures given by RAF in 1940	Figures given by RAF after war	Figures in German High Command Diary
15 August	185	76	55
18 August	155	71	49
15 September	185	56	50
27 September	153	55	42
Totals	678	258	196

The **British Expeditionary Force**, which had been sent to help the French, was forced to join them in retreat. Soon more than 300,000 Allied troops were penned in around the port of Dunkirk. Hitler ordered Goering, the Commander of the *Luftwaffe*, to use his bombers to destroy these forces.

Britain launched a desperate effort to rescue the soldiers. The government appealed for help to get them off the beaches. Between 24 May and 4 June an armada of hundreds of small, privately owned boats sailed to France and helped the Royal Navy to ferry nearly 330,000 French and English troops to larger ships offshore. The Dunkirk rescue has become one of the most famous events in British history. Even today great bravery in the face of overwhelming odds is often referred to as the 'Dunkirk spirit'.

Within a month of the Dunkirk evacuation France surrendered to Germany. Instead of occupying the whole of France, Germany allowed southern France to set up a government run by General Pétain at **Vichy**. The **Vichy Government** was really controlled by the Germans. However, it was run by the French themselves – Hitler hoped that this would stop the French colonies and navy from going over to the British side.

Britain braced itself for an invasion, but Hitler knew that before he could invade he would have to destroy the **Royal Air Force** (RAF). Between July and September 1940 the RAF and the German *Luftwaffe* fought the '**Battle of Britain**' in the skies over England. The British came perilously close to defeat, but managed to fight off the German attacks. On 17 September Hitler abandoned his planned invasion. Instead he decided to bomb Britain's cities. From autumn 1940 until spring 1941 wave after wave of German bombers attacked London and other main centres of population and industrial production. But like the Battle of Britain, Hitler's 'Blitz' proved unsuccessful. Britain continued to stand firm.

Numbers of German aircraft shot down on four days during the Battle of Britain in 1940.

Pétain

Henri Philippe Pétain (1856–1951) was a French First World War hero, who was later sentenced to death for treason. He was educated at St Cyr military college and became a colonel in 1912. After he won a famous victory against the Germans at Verdun in 1916, he was appointed Commander-in-Chief of the French forces on the Western Front. When the Germans occupied northern France in the Second World War, Pétain became head of the Vichy government, which ruled unoccupied France. But after the Germans overran Vichy in France in 1942, he became little more than a puppet ruler. At the end of the war he was condemned to death for treason, but his sentence was reduced to life imprisonment.

4.2 The German Invasion of the USSR

Despite the signing of the Nazi–Soviet Pact in 1939, Germany and the USSR remained bitter rivals. Hitler saw the Slav people of the USSR as **Untermenschen** (sub-humans) and detested Communism. He wanted to conquer the USSR and take control of its valuable oil fields and fertile wheat plains. A defeated USSR would also provide *Lebensraum* for German settlers. The Soviet people could then be put to work as slave labourers.

Hitler had planned to invade the USSR in spring 1941. But **'Operation Barbarossa'**, as the Germans called the attack, did not actually take place until 22 June. Hitler had to spend the spring of that year rescuing his Italian ally, Mussolini, from the difficulties he had got into during his invasion of Greece. This delay proved to be vitally important.

When the invasion was finally launched the Germans soon drove deep into Soviet territory. Their Panzer tank units advanced up to 32 km a day. By November the Germans were threatening Moscow, Leningrad and Kiev. What Hitler had not expected, however, was that his troops would still be fighting when winter came. The temperature in the USSR rarely rises above freezing point from late November to early April, and the Germans were totally unprepared for the severity of such weather. At the end of November their advance came to a halt as oil froze in the tanks. Equipped only with summer uniforms, more than 1,000,000 of the German troops suffered from frostbite. They were also short of supplies, as the retreating Soviets had adopted a **'scorched earth'** policy, destroying anything which they could not carry away.

As the Germans dug in for the winter, the better equipped Soviets launched a series of counter-offensives, led by Marshal Zhukov. They also moved over 1500 arms and munitions factories deep into the eastern USSR. There they would be safe from the Germans. By the end of 1942 these factories were pouring out weapons for the army. Help was coming from abroad, too, as Britain and later the USA sent tanks and aircraft.

A

SOURCE

A German soldier using a flame-thrower during an attack on a Soviet village.

B

SOURCE

Rifles became so cold that if a man picked his up with a bare hand, it stuck to the rifle. It was so cold that he didn't realize what had happened. So when he took his hand away, he found that the flesh of the palm and fingers remained on the rifle. It was the height of danger to urinate in the open; men were literally and permanently unmanned for being so rash.

The effects of the cold in the USSR. From R. Seth, 'Operation Barabarossa', 1964.

The Germans continued their advance when spring came. Their main aim was to capture the oilfields of the Caucasus region. But when they reached **Stalingrad** Hitler ordered his Sixth Army to take the city. This was to prove a mistake. The Soviets were prepared to stake everything to hold the city. They also proved more effective at the kind of street fighting that was involved in what became known as the **Battle of Stalingrad**.

In November fresh Soviet troops arrived and the Germans found themselves surrounded. Despite Hitler's orders that he should fight on, **Von Paulus**, the Commander of the Sixth Army, surrendered in February 1943. The remaining German forces began a long and miserable retreat towards home. The invasion of the USSR had proved to be a terrible mistake for Hitler. It had cost Germany nearly 200,000 men. But the USSR had suffered even greater losses. Nearly 20 million Soviet soldiers and civilians had died defending their homeland.

C

SOURCE

A Soviet cartoon from the Second World War showing Hitler ordering his troops to their death.

The German attack on the USSR, 1941–2.

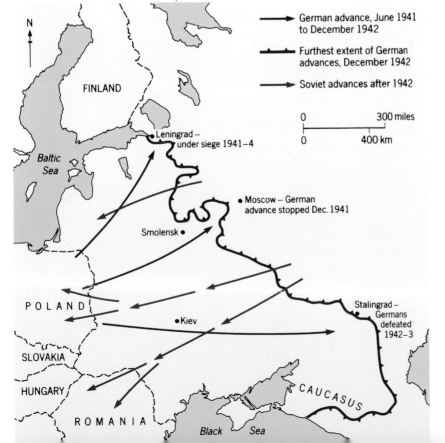

N

FINLAND

→ German advance, June 1941 to December 1942

▲ Furthest extent of German advances, December 1942

→ Soviet advances after 1942

0   300 miles
0   400 km

Baltic Sea

Leningrad – under siege 1941–4

• Moscow – German advance stopped Dec. 1941

Smolensk •

POLAND

• Kiev

Stalingrad – Germans defeated 1942–3

SLOVAKIA

HUNGARY

CAUCASUS

ROMANIA

Black Sea

Zhukov

Georgi Zhukov (1896–1974) was the USSR's leading Second World War general. After the First World War he became an expert on the use of tanks. In the Second World War Zhukov led the defence of Leningrad in 1941 and raised the German siege of Stalingrad in 1942. He commanded the Soviet forces which advanced into Germany and captured Berlin in May 1945. After the war he became Minister of Defence under Khrushchev. He retired in 1957.

4.3 Europe under the Nazis

By the end of 1942 Nazi Germany controlled almost all of Europe and was opposed only by the USSR and Britain. All other European countries were either neutral or allied to Germany. The Nazis exploited the lands they controlled for their own use. Local resources, such as Polish coal, were used in the German war effort. Many factories were taken over and put to work making goods for Germany. Some were simply closed down and their valuable machinery shipped home to be used in German factories. Food, too, was taken from conquered countries and transported to German soldiers and civilians. The Nazis were not concerned if this caused starvation to the population of the country from which the food was taken.

Perhaps the major resource exploited by the Germans was **labour**. To produce the food and goods needed to win the war Germany had to find millions of extra workers for its farms and factories. The answer was to use slave labour. By 1944 there were more than seven million slave workers in Germany. About half of these were from the USSR. The Germans treated prisoners of war from western Europe well, since most of them were **Aryans**, like the Germans (see Unit 4.8). Those from eastern Europe were generally **Slavs**, people whom Hitler saw as sub-human and not worthy of respect. Germany took more than five million Soviet soldiers prisoner during the war. Many were transported to Germany as slave labour.

A SOURCE

Of 3,600,000 Soviet prisoners, only a few hundred thousand are still able to work fully. Camp commanders have forbidden food to be put at their disposal, instead they have let them starve to death. Even on the way to the work camps civilians were not allowed to give the prisoners food. If prisoners could not keep up, they were shot before the eyes of horrified civilians.

Letter from the Nazi minister in charge of the German-occupied USSR, February 1942.

Europe at the end of 1942.

Germany
Occupied areas
German allies
Neutral countries

0   300 miles
0   400 km

Not everything that the Nazis took was to help them win the war. As they occupied land, they took many of the most valuable paintings, sculptures and other art treasures. Many of these found their way back to Germany. Goering, in particular, amassed a valuable collection of stolen art treasures.

The harshness of German rule varied according to the status of the conquered countries. In the west the Germans took control using local politicians if possible. In Norway Major Quisling took charge. In France General Pétain headed the Vichy Government. But the Germans always made sure their rule was obeyed. Anyone who opposed the Nazis was dealt with either by the **Gestapo** (the secret police) or the **SS** (an organization of 'elite' troops which was used to control opposition to Hitler). The SS was also responsible for running the concentration camps.

In eastern Europe, however, the Nazis planned to clear the population to make *Lebensraum* for German settlers. Jews were transported to the death camps (see Unit 4.8); millions of other eastern Europeans were sent to work as slave labour in Germany. In the USSR special 'action groups' followed behind the German army. Their target was to kill civilians and prisoners-of-war in territory won by the Nazis. Over a million people died in this way. It was little wonder that Soviet soldiers sometimes treated German civilians with brutality when they advanced into Nazi Germany.

Goering

Hermann Goering (1893–1946) joined the Nazi Party shortly after its foundation and was wounded in the Munich *Putsch of 1923*. Hitler appointed him Air Minister in 1933. In 1936 he began to prepare Germany's air force for war. In 1940 Hitler gave him the special title of 'Reichsmarshall'. He began to lose influence after Germany's failure to defeat Britain. He is said to have amassed a private fortune from war booty and to have been a drug addict. He was found guilty of war crimes at the Nuremberg trials and committed suicide.

German soldiers hanging Soviet citizens.

B

SOURCE

4.4 Opposition to the Nazis

Opposition within Germany

At the outbreak of war Hitler was popular in Germany. He had brought prosperity to Germany and re-occupied the lands taken in the hated Versailles Treaty. Most people were quite prepared to accept the restrictions that Nazi rule brought. They did not like the banning of opposition political parties and trade unions, or the persecution of the Jews, but this seemed an acceptable price to pay for Hitler's brilliant successes in foreign policy. Goebbel's clever use of **propaganda** (see Unit 4.9) also helped persuade Germans that all was well.

There were some people whose conscience refused to allow them to support what Hitler was doing. Some of these people would not join the army; others spoke out against Nazi policies. Such behaviour led to arrest and often execution. By 1939 Hitler had crushed most of the opposition, but there were still some Germans who were prepared to work to overthrow him. If caught, these people were shown no mercy. In 1944 a group of army leaders decided that Hitler was leading Germany to defeat. They tried to assassinate him, but their bomb plot failed. They were tortured and then hanged with piano wire.

Resistance movements

In countries occupied by Germany there were groups of people who were prepared to carry on an **underground war** against the Nazis. These were members of the **Resistance**. They played an important role in undermining the German war effort by sabotaging railways, bridges and factories. They kept up people's morale by secretly producing pamphlets and newspapers urging their countrymen and women to carry on the fight.

Although resistance groups existed in all occupied countries, the most famous is the French **Maquis**. It helped to organize escape routes for Allied airmen who had been shot down, carried out bombings of factories and disrupted German communications during the D-Day landings.

Letter home from an imprisoned German agricultural worker.

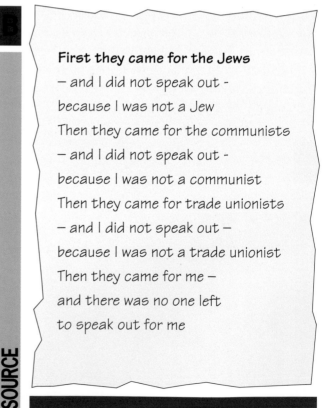

A poem written by the German churchman, Pastor Niemoller, during his imprisonment by the Nazis.

SOURCE

How to take a photograph in secret. The woman apparently fumbling in her bag, has a hidden camera (the lens can be seen just below the centre of the two rings).

D

SOURCE

Within weeks of being put in charge, Heydrich arrested nearly 5000 Czech resistance workers. Most of them were executed. Yet this did not stop the sabotage. According to German sources, war production in Czech factories went down by 33%. Heydrich said that he had not done his job properly.

Dr. J. L Charles, 'Europe's Secret Armies', 1966.

In Czechoslovakia the Resistance assassinated the SS General Reynhard Heydrich. Nazi retaliation was severe. In the Czech village of Lidice all 192 males were shot, 82 children sent to the gas chambers, 35 older women sent to Auschwitz death camp (see Unit 4.8) and the remaining women put in a labour camp. Even the dogs were shot in their kennels. Then Lidice was burned to the ground.

At first Britain did not provide much help to the resistance groups. But the British soon realized how valuable these groups were not only for undermining the German war effort, but also for providing vital information for the Allies. Therefore in 1940 the British formed the **Special Operations Executive** to co-ordinate the work of the various resistance groups. SOE agents were smuggled into occupied areas to give support to the local fighters.

Heydrich

Reinhard Heydrich (1904–42) was Hitler's number two during the Second World War. Unlike most of the other leaders, he resembled the 'Aryan' perfection which Hitler wanted, having blonde hair and blue eyes.

Heydrich was made head of the Gestapo in 1936. In 1941 he took charge of the policy of transporting Jews from all parts of Europe to the concentration camps. Some historians believe that he could have been Hitler's successor, but in 1942 he was assassinated by Czech partisans.

4.5 War in the Pacific

By the end of 1941 the Second World War had spread to the **Pacific**. As we saw in Unit 3.3, after 1929 Japan was facing economic difficulties which it believed could only be solved by winning new territory.

Following its invasion of Manchuria Japan began devising a plan for 'New Order' in Asia. It said that the time had come for the Europeans and Americans to be expelled and for the **Greater Asia Co-Prosperity Plan** to be put into operation. This involved setting up an organization under Japan's leadership to provide economic growth and political independence. In reality it meant Japan gaining control of Asia and exploiting its raw materials for Japan's own use.

Japan faced strong opposition from the Americans. The USA had been concerned about the growth of Japanese power ever since the First World War. It was not prepared to see Japan build an empire in South-East Asia and threaten US trade. So, in 1940, the USA imposed a total **embargo** (block) on the sale of oil to Japan. Since 80% of Japan's oil came from the USA, it would be just a matter of time before Japanese industries ground to a halt.

By 1941 the Japanese had come to the conclusion that they needed to take military action to seize control of the raw materials of Asia. Britain and Holland had colonies in Asia, but they were too busy fighting Germany to be able to protect their possessions in the East. What *would* be a problem for the Japanese was the power of the US Navy, which could prevent any Japanese take-over. The Japanese therefore decided on a surprise attack to destroy the US Pacific fleet at **Pearl Harbor**, Hawaii. Then they could take over South-East Asia before the Americans rebuilt their navy.

SOURCE A

A Dutch poster printed in England during the Second World War. It says, 'The Indies must be freed. Work and fight for it!' Before the war the East Indies were part of the Dutch Empire.

The attack came at 8 am on Sunday 7 December 1941. Japanese aircraft swept down on the US base. They destroyed eight battleships and more than 350 planes. They also killed 2400 Americans. But they did not totally destroy the US fleet as they had hoped. Instead they 'awoke a sleeping giant'. The USA immediately declared war on Japan, and on Japan's allies, Germany and Italy. Within two years the Americans had rebuilt their fleet and gone on the attack against Japan. By that time, however, the Japanese had achieved their aim of winning control of much of South-East Asia.

On Christmas Day 1941 the Japanese captured the British base of **Hong Kong**. They took two US bases, **Guam** and **Wake**, before the year was over. Early in 1942 the Japanese marched through **Malaya** and in February captured the great British naval base at **Singapore**. This was to be Britain's worst defeat of the whole war, with 80,000 troops taken prisoner. In March 1942 the Japanese captured **Java**, followed rapidly by the rest of the **Dutch East Indies**. **Burma** (a British colony) fell in April and the **Philippines** (USA) in May. By July 1942 much of **New Guinea** had been captured and **Australia** was under threat from the Japanese.

Japan had set up its 'New Order' in South-East Asia, but could it defend it against the might of the USA?

B SOURCE

The Allied soldiers found it very difficult to cope with jungle conditions. Unlike the rice-eating Japanese, they suffered through inadequate diet and fell victim to a variety of tropical diseases. The humidity and heat, combined with the problem of mosquitoes, meant that every day large numbers of men were unfit for combat.

Problems encountered by Allied soldiers fighting in the Pacific area. From N. Kelly, 'The Second World War', 1989.

MacArthur

Douglas MacArthur (1880–1964) attended the famous army college at West Point. He fought in the First World War and showed great skill as an officer. After the war he became Superintendent of West Point and in 1932 was sent to break up Washington's 'Hoovervilles' (shanty towns of homeless unemployed people). He retired in1937 but he was called out of retirement to try to stop the Japanese occupation of the Philippines. He led the campaign against the Japanese and received their surrender in September 1945. MacArthur commanded the UN troops in the Korean War until he was sacked by President Truman in 1951.

The war in the Pacific, 1941–2.

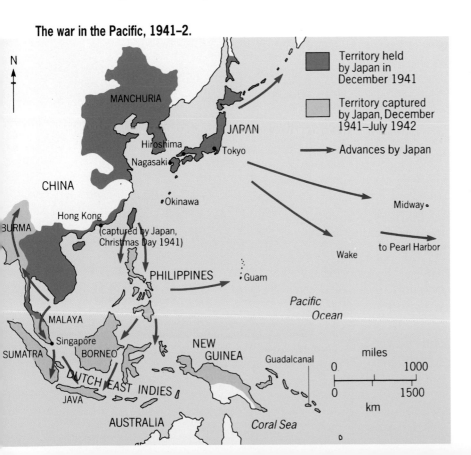

Territory held by Japan in December 1941

Territory captured by Japan, December 1941–July 1942

Advances by Japan

4.6 The Allied Victories in the West

At the beginning of 1941, Hitler's Germany seemed in a very strong position. Only Britain stood between Hitler and victory. But by 1942 the situation had changed dramatically. In June 1941 Hitler launched his ill-fated attack on the USSR, and in December the USA entered the war. By 1945 the Allies were so strong that Germany's defeat was unavoidable.

The North African Front

In Africa, Britain was fighting Italian and German forces for control of the Mediterranean coast and the Suez Canal. The British defeated the Italians, but found the German forces under **Field Marshal Rommel** much harder to beat. However, a new British commander, **General Montgomery**, led the British to a decisive victory at **El Alamein** in October 1942. When US forces arrived to help in November 1942, the Allies began to push the Italians and Germans out of Africa. Then, in July 1943, they invaded Sicily and began to march through Italy towards Germany.

The Soviet Front

After their defeat at Stalingrad in 1942, the Germans suffered further defeats in 1943 and 1944. Their glorious campaign became a desperate retreat. By July 1944 the Soviet forces had pushed them back into Poland. By April 1945 they had liberated eastern Europe from German control. In May they reached Berlin.

The Western Front

By 1944 the Allies were ready to launch an attack on Hitler in Europe. On 6 June – D-Day – Allied forces under the command of the US General Eisenhower landed on five beaches in Normandy. By the end of that day they had managed to establish themselves, and supplies and reinforcements began arriving from across the English Channel. Then the Allies began advancing across France. By September northern France, Luxembourg and Belgium had been liberated. General de Gaulle, who had established himself as leader of the 'Free French' while in exile in London, returned to Paris to head the government.

B SOURCE

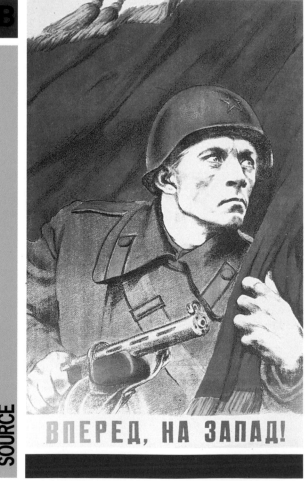

ВПЕРЕД, НА ЗАПАД!

A Second World War poster encouraging Soviet forces to victory over the Germans.

Meanwhile the Allies pressed on. They overcame a German counter attack in December 1944 (the **Battle of the Bulge**) and reached Berlin in April 1945.

The bombing campaign

From 1942 the Allies launched a series of **bombing raids** on Germany. Sir Arthur ('Bomber') Harris organized 'thousand bomber' raids which caused havoc in German cities and destroyed industrial sites. In one raid alone, at Dresden in February 1945, 135,000 Germans died. By April 1945 much of Berlin had been turned to rubble and its people were starving.

By the end of April 1945 Germany was on the point of collapse. On 30 April Hitler and his wife, Eva Braun, committed suicide in his bunker under Berlin. Admiral Doenitz assumed command and surrendered to the Allies on 7 May.

Montgomery

Field Marshall Bernard Law Montgomery (1887–1976) was the British soldier sent to Africa to command the Eighth Army in 1942. He won a spectacular victory over the German forces led by Field Marshall Rommel at El Alamein which led to British control of North Africa. Montgomery was one of the commanders of the Allied forces during the D-Day landings of 6 June 1944.

The defeat of Germany.

4.7 Victory in the Pacific

By late 1942 the Japanese had captured much of South-East Asia, but there were signs that the tide was already beginning to turn. In the spring of 1942 the US Navy won victories at **Coral Sea** and **Midway Island**. The US fleet now dominated the Pacific Ocean.

American forces then began the process of recapturing Japan's conquests. Their plan of attack was based on 'island-hopping'. The aim was to leap-frog across the Pacific, island by island, until they reached Japan. Their first reconquest was **Guadalcanal** in August 1942. But it cost more than 1600 US lives. The Americans discovered that the Japanese were fanatical fighters. They considered surrender to be dishonourable and believed that soldiers should fight to the death. This made them very difficult to defeat, even when they were faced with heavy losses. For example, 24,000 Japanese soldiers were killed defending Guadalcanal.

During 1943 and 1944 the Americans managed to recapture one Pacific island after another, often inflicting heavy losses on the Japanese. In June 1944 the Japanese lost 480 planes and three aircraft carriers at the **Battle of the Philippine Sea**. Almost 170,000 Japanese soldiers died when the Americans re-captured the Philippines. In June the Americans took **Okinawa**, an island just 650 kilometres to the south of Japan.

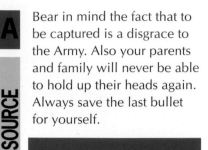

A **SOURCE**
Bear in mind the fact that to be captured is a disgrace to the Army. Also your parents and family will never be able to hold up their heads again. Always save the last bullet for yourself.

Extract from the Japanese Army Manual issued during the war.

B
'My God, what have we done?'

Captain R. Lewis, co-pilot of the Enola Gay on seeing the effects of the bomb.

C
'This is the greatest thing in history.'

US President Truman, on being told of the dropping of the bomb.

D **SOURCE**

The city of Hiroshima after the dropping of the atomic bomb.

The Japanese were so determined not to give in that they were literally prepared to commit suicide. **Kamikaze** or suicide pilots would volunteer for missions in which they became 'living bombs'. The pilot would take off in an obsolete plane, packed with explosives, then fly directly at a US warship. When the US forces attacked Okinawa, some 2000 Kamikaze pilots died, sinking 30 US warships.

By mid-1945 the Japanese were in a desperate position. Since 1944 US bombers had flown unchallenged over Japan. They dropped many incendiary bombs which caused dreadful destruction to Japanese cities. On 15 March 80,000 Japanese died in a bombing raid on the city of Tokyo. This was more people than had been killed in the whole of England during the Blitz. Japan had also been cut off from its supplies of raw materials, and a US blockade was resulting in widespread food shortages. In Burma, Japanese forces were also being defeated by the British.

By the end of July 1945, the Japanese government asked the USSR to approach the US government to see if terms for surrender could be agreed. However, US President Truman was convinced that Japan's surrender must be unconditional. So the Japanese forces continued to fight. Truman was faced with the problem of how to defeat the Japanese without the enormous loss of US life that an invasion would bring.

The answer seemed to lie in the new weapon that US scientists had developed. This was the **atomic bomb**. Tests had shown that it was capable of destroying whole cities. If one of these bombs were to be dropped on a Japanese city, it would surely cause them to surrender. Truman sent the Japanese an ultimatum demanding unconditional surrender. The Japanese ignored the ultimatum.

At 8.15 am on 6 August 1945 the US bomber *Enola Gay* flew over the city of **Hiroshima**. Colonel Tibbets released the bomb. The massive explosion destroyed the city. Over 80,000 civilians died from the explosion – many more died later from the effects of radiation. Incredibly, the Japanese still did not surrender. On 9 August a further bomb was dropped on **Nagasaki**, killing 40,000 Japanese. On the same day the USSR invaded Japanese-held Manchuria. Now the Japanese had no choice. Emperor Hirohito broadcast the news of Japan's surrender on 15 August 1945. The war was over.

My daughter had no burns and only minor external wounds. However, on 4 September she suddenly became sick. She had spots all over her body. Her hair began to fall out. She vomited small clumps of blood many times. After ten days of agony she died.

A Hiroshima father's account of his daughter's death.

Einstein

Albert Einstein (1879–1955) was a German Jew who fled Germany to avoid persecution. He was born at Ulm in Germany and moved to Switzerland at the age of 15. While working in Basle in 1905 he began to develop his Theory of Relativity, which is the basis of atomic power. After a time as Professor in Zurich and Prague, Einstein returned to Germany and in 1921 won the Nobel Prize for Physics.

In 1933 he fled to the USA to avoid Nazi persecution. He became worried that his work could be used to develop an atomic bomb. In 1939 he warned President Roosevelt of the danger to world peace if Nazi Germany developed such a bomb. He was so concerned that he tried unsuccessfully to have the United Nations take control of atomic energy.

4.8 The Holocaust

Throughout history the **Jews** have been persecuted. They were often expelled from countries in the Middle Ages and have been victims of racial attacks in many countries during the 20th century. Yet despite thousands of years of persecution, the Jews have never experienced such dreadful treatment as they received at the hands of Hitler's Nazis.

In 1920 Adolf Hitler set out the views of the new Nazi Party. The people of Germany and northern Europe were members of the same 'Aryan' race. He believed that this race was the 'master race' born to rule over all the other races. The Jews, on the other hand, were an inferior people who polluted the pure Aryan race. Worse than this, the Nazis claimed that the Jews had intrigued with the Communists at the end of the First World War and in some unexplained way were responsible for Germany's defeat. Since the war, the Nazis said, the Jews had continued to work to undermine the German government. They were to blame for nearly all that was wrong with Germany.

At first people took little notice of Hitler's extreme views. After all, many Jews had fought with great bravery in the German armed forces in the war. Yet slowly but surely the Nazis began to win support. In January 1933 Hitler became Chancellor (leader of the German government). Now he had a chance to put his anti-Jewish ideas into practice.

The Nazis used school education to spread their anti-Jewish views. Children were taught to be proud to be Aryans and not to mix with Jews. Pupils even had lessons on how their own race was superior to all others. Jewish children were often ridiculed in front of their classmates.

The worst treatment, however, was given to adults. It began with people attacking Jewish shops or simply refusing to buy things from them. Sometimes Nazi soldiers stood outside to prevent people entering. In April 1933 all Jews working in the German civil service were thrown out of their jobs.

A SOURCE

A Nazi poster: 'We peasants are clearing out the muck'. The 'muck' shown is a group of Communists and Jews.

B 9.40–10.25 : Monday to Saturday: either Race Study or Ideology.

Extract from a German school timetable during the Nazi period.

C SOURCE

When I went to school at the age of 10, a third of my classmates were Jewish girls. I got on well with them, just as well as with all the others. From the older generation we learned that the Jews were wicked and that they would help Germany's enemies if there were a war.

Memories of a German woman who was a schoolgirl in the Nazi period.

In 1935 local authorities banned Jews from swimming baths, parks and playing fields. They were also deprived of their right to vote. In the same year the **Nuremberg Laws** banned marriage between Jews and non-Jews. It also became illegal for Jews and non-Jews who were not married to have sexual intercourse.

From 1938 the persecution of Jews was stepped up. When a German diplomat was murdered by a Jew in Paris, the Nazis carried out revenge attacks on German Jews. On 9 November 1938, over 7000 Jewish shops were attacked and synagogues and homes burned down. More than 30,000 Jews were rounded up and sent to concentration camps. This night has since been labelled **Kristallnacht** (Crystal Night). One leading Nazi complained about the cost to insurance companies. He said, 'they should have killed more Jews and broken less glass.'

Kristallnacht was the final straw for many Jews. Those who could get away joined the stream of Jews fleeing from Germany. For those who were unable to leave, a terrible fate was in store.

E

SOURCE

In 1934 a Berlin schoolboy interrupted his teacher's anti-Jewish lecture with the remark, 'My daddy says Jews are not damnably vile.' His daddy was put in prison.

From T. Howarth 'The World Since 1900', 1979.

Eichmann

Karl Adolf Eichmann (1906–62) was born in Austria. He joined the German Nazi Party and became a member of the SS. From 1939 he was Chief of the Gestapo's Jewish section, a post he particularly enjoyed as he was a well-known anti-Semite. He was a strong supporter of the policy of using gas chambers to kill Jews.

At the end of the war he was captured by US forces, but managed to keep his identity secret. He escaped from prison in 1945 and reached Argentina, where a number of other Nazi leaders were in hiding. In 1950 he was kidnapped by Israeli agents and taken to Israel to face charges of 'crimes against humanity'. He was found guilty and executed.

D

SOURCE

A cartoon showing anti-Jewish studies at school. The students are being taught to recognize Jewish 'characteristics'.

By the end of 1941 the Nazis had taken control of much of Europe. During this time they had conquered lands where millions of Jews lived. Many of these Jews were herded into **ghettoes** in the cities where they lived in such appalling conditions that starvation was common. Others were sent to **concentration camps** where they were put to work beside other 'undesirables' such as pacifists, communists, gypsies and homosexuals.

In 1941 Hitler devised his **Final Solution** to the Jewish 'problem'. A series of death camps was to be set up to carry out a mass slaughter of the whole Jewish population of Europe. During the next four years the Nazis were responsible for the deaths of over six million Jews in what has become known as the **Holocaust**.

Various methods were used to kill the Jews. Special death camps were set up to carry out the task. Sometimes the Jews were lined up alongside huge graves and shot so that they fell in. But as so many were to be killed, the Germans had to find more efficient ways of extermination. The method they chose was Cyclon B poison gas crystals. As many as 2000 people could be killed at one time. The victims were led into huge chambers, which were then sealed. The gas was released and after about three minutes everyone was dead. Then the bodies were taken away and burned. Useful by-products, like gold teeth, glasses and hair were kept for use by the Nazis. Other concentration camp inmates were used for medical experiments carried out without anaesthetic. This usually resulted in the death of the patient.

The Führer has ordered the Jewish question to be settled once and for all. The Jews are sworn enemies of the German people and must be eradicated. Every Jew that we can lay our hands on is to be destroyed now, during the war, without exception.

An account from the memoirs of Rudolf Hoess, Commandant of Auschwitz, telling how he was ordered to begin the extermination of the Jews.

Then the prisoner guards had to find the small children who had been hidden. They opened the doors of the gas chamber and threw all the children in. 'Oh!' I said, 'I've never seen anything like it in my life. It's absolutely terrible.' My guide said, 'You get used to anything after a while.'

An SS officer's reaction on first witnessing the gassing of the Jews, recalled in a television interview in the 1960s.

The main concentration camps.

The Germans issued propaganda films showing good conditions in the camps. This encouraged many people to believe that reports of atrocities were exaggerated. After the liberation of the territory around camps such as **Auschwitz**, **Maidenek** and **Chelmno**, Britain and France could no longer pretend that they didn't know what was happening.

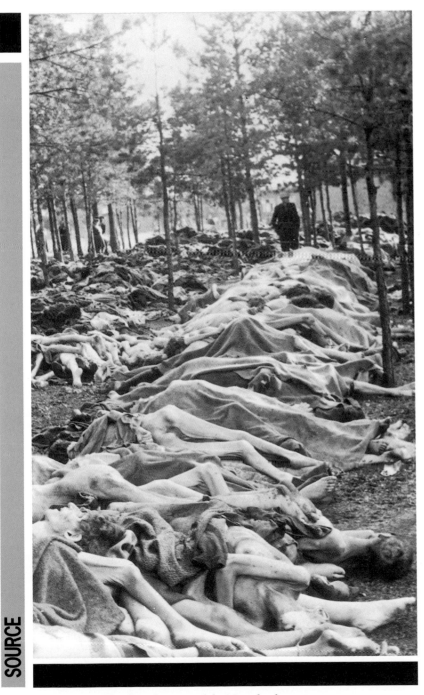

SOURCE

So far three million have died. It is the greatest mass-killing in recorded history: and it goes on daily, hourly, as regularly as the ticking of your watch. I have been lecturing Allied troops for three years now and their attitude is always the same. They don't believe it.

Arthur Koestler, an American journalist, writing in the 'New York Times' in January 1944.

SOURCE

Rows of corpses awaiting burial at one of the Nazi death camps.

Himmler

Heinrich Himmler (1900–45) was one of the most ruthless Nazi leaders. His career was a series of successes. In 1927 he became the deputy leader of the SS. He took over as leader in 1929 and later, in 1936, he became a commander of the entire Nazi police force. His final promotion came in 1943 when he was made Minister of the Interior. Himmler set up the death camps for exterminating the Jews and, as head of the SS, he was responsible for carrying out the policy. He did so with a ruthless determination which made him a hated figure.

After the defeat of Germany he tried to escape in disguise but he was spotted by the British on 21 May 1945. Two days after his capture, he committed suicide.

4.9 Civilians at War: A Study in Depth

In 1918 people talked of how the First World War was 'the war to end all wars'. Unfortunately, they were soon to be proved wrong. What is perhaps more accurate is that the First World War was limited almost entirely to the troops taking part in the fighting. The Second World War saw the beginning of total warfare, which involved both military forces and civilians. Technological advances meant that bombers could now fly deep into enemy territory to attack both military and civilian targets. This depth study looks at how the war affected civilians.

The Blitz

In September 1940 Hitler postponed his planned invasion of Britain. But while he might not be able to invade, he could still bomb. If he could cause sufficient terror in Britain's cities, then perhaps the British people would call upon Prime Minister Churchill to accept defeat. So Hitler ordered the *Luftwaffe* to launch a series of bombing raids on Britain's major cities.

The raids began on 7 September. London was bombed on 75 of the next 76 days. Perhaps the worst single raid on a British city came on 14 November 1940. Coventry suffered a ten-hour bombardment which destroyed one-third of the city and killed more than 4000 civilians. **The Blitz** continued until early summer 1941. Over 40,000 civilians were killed and more than two million people made homeless.

The government took a number of steps to try to protect civilians. It ordered a total **blackout**. All windows had to be covered by thick blackout curtains. Street and vehicle lights were shielded or dimmed. It was an offence to 'show a light' that might guide a German bomber to its target.

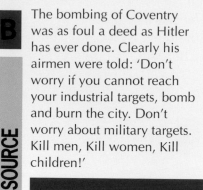

SOURCE B

The bombing of Coventry was as foul a deed as Hitler has ever done. Clearly his airmen were told: 'Don't worry if you cannot reach your industrial targets, bomb and burn the city. Don't worry about military targets. Kill men, Kill women, Kill children!'

From the 'Daily Herald', 16 November 1940.

SOURCE A

How much sleep did you get last night?

| None 31% | Less than 4 hours 32% | 4–6 hours 22% | More than 6 hours 15% |

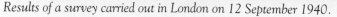

Results of a survey carried out in London on 12 September 1940.

SOURCE

The centre of Canterbury after heavy bombing.

SOURCE

A bus in a bomb crater caused by a raid in the Balham area of London, 1940.

Everyone was issued with a gas mask, in case the Germans dropped gas bombs. Windows were taped up to avoid flying splinters. Important buildings were protected by sandbags. Some people erected Anderson bomb shelters in their gardens, or used Morrison shelters indoors. In towns, there were public shelters where people could go if the air-raid warning sounded. In London, some families decided that the safest place to spend the night was on the platforms of the London Underground.

Harris

'Bomber' Harris (1892–1984) was born in Cheltenham, Gloucestershire and emigrated to Zimbabwe at the age of 10. During the First World War he fought the Germans in south-west Africa as a member of the 1st Rhodesian Regiment and later joined the Royal Flying Corps operating on the Western Front in France. He became a squadron leader in the newly formed RAF in 1918 and was promoted to Air Commodore in 1937. During the Second World War he became Deputy Chief of Air. This gave him the opportunity to put into operation his beliefs that the war could be more easily won by bombing enemy cities. In January 1943 he was given orders to disrupt German industry by a bombing campaign. Any German city with a population of over 100,000 inhabitants was considered to be a fair target. The bombing raids caused terrible destruction. On 13 February 1945 there were 135,000 casualties after a raid on Dresden in Germany. In 1992 a statue was erected in London in honour of the role played by Harris in helping Britain win the war.

From Blitz to Atomic Wipeout

The 'Blitz' on Britain's major cities represented the first sustained aerial bombardment of civilian populations. But the German raids did not break the will of the British and soon the boot was on the other foot. At the start of the war the British had been reluctant to carry out attacks which threatened to produce large numbers of civilian casualties. From 1942, however, 'Bomber' Harris helped co-ordinate attacks on any German cities with populations of over 100,000. Dresden was particularly hard hit. These raids caused terrible devastation but are considered to have made a significant contribution to helping the Allies win the war.

But the bombing raids have also been criticized for taking the lives of hundreds of thousands of innocent women and children. The severest criticism has been reserved for the Americans. The US Air Force played a significant part in the bombing of Germany and, in Japan, reduced many Japanese cities to rubble (see Unit 4.7). In August 1945, President Truman decided that the only way to end the war without the loss of hundreds of thousands of American soldiers lives was by dropping atomic bombs on Japan. The bombs which hit Hiroshima and Nagasaki brought the end of the war nearer but cost over 120,000 Japanese lives.

Victims of allied bombing in Dresden, February 1945

SOURCE

Dresden by this time has become the main centre of communications defence of Germany. It was also the largest city in Germany which had been left intact; it had never been bombed before. As a large centre of war industry it was also of the highest importance.

Sir Arthur Harris, who was in charge of Bomber Command from 1942 to 1945 explains why he considered Dresden a fair target.

SOURCE

It struck me at the time, the thought of women and children down there. We seemed to fly for hours over a sheet of fire – a terrific red glow with thin haze over it. I found myself making comments to the crew, 'Oh God, those poor people'. It was completely uncalled for. You can't justify it.

The views of an RAF pilot who took part in the bombing of Dresden.

Bombs dropped on Britain and Germany 1940–45 (in tons)		
Year	**Britain**	**Germany**
1940	37,000	10,000
1941	21,000	30,000
1942	3,000	40,000
1943	9,000	120,000
1944	2,000	650,000
1945	750	500,000

Bombing during the Second World War.

Stacked up corpses were being hauled away on lorries. Everywhere there was the stench of the dead and the smoke. I saw places on the pavement where people had been roasted to death. At last I comprehended first-hand what an air-raid meant. I turned back, sick and scared. Later I learned that there had been 100,000 casualties and 375,000 left homeless.

Memories of a Japanese girl who experienced the bombing raids on Tokyo in March 1945.

The impact of the bomb was so terrific that practically all living things, human and animal, were literally seared to death by the tremendous heat and pressure engendered by the blast. Buildings were crushed or wiped out. The city is a disastrous ruin.

Radio Tokyo after the atomic bombing of Hiroshima in Japan.

The engineer director of the atomic project was desperate to see the fruits of the project's labours before the end of the war. The military equipment was available and had been developed at a cost of $2,000 million. It would have been difficult to justify not using it after such a vast financial investment. Truman was very impressed with what we heard and believed, along with most of his advisors that if the bomb could be built it should be used. For some reason the scientists failed to mention the long term dangers of radiation.
Both bombs were atomic bombs. The Nagasaki bomb produced a greater blast. Some of the leaders of the project were keen for both bombs to be tested. Nagasaki was, in short, an experiment.

From an article in the magazine of the Campaign for Nuclear Disarmament published in 1985.

All of us realised that the fighting in Japan would be fierce and had been estimated that it might cost half a million American lives to force the enemy's surrender on his home ground. I had realised that an atomic bomb explosion would inflict damage and casualties beyond imagination, but my scientific advisors told me that they could not put on a technical demonstration and that there was no alternative to direct military use. When I talked to Prime Minister Churchill he unhesitatingly told me that he favoured the use of the atomic bomb if it might aid to end the war.

From the memoirs of President Truman, who ordered the dropping of atomic bombs on Hiroshima and Nagasaki.

Churchill

Winston Churchill (1874–1965) is remembered as one of Britain`s greatest wartime Prime Ministers.

He was born in Blenheim, Oxfordshire, the son of a wealthy landowner. He was educated at Harrow public school and Sandhurst Military Academy.

He joined the army and took part in the Battle of Omdurman in 1898. In 1900 he became a Conservative MP, but left to join the Liberal Party in 1904. In 1910 he became Home Secretary and in 1911 First Lord of the Admiralty.

By 1924 he had rejoined the Conservative Party and was again elected as a Conservative MP. He was Chancellor of the Exchequer from 1924–9 and in 1939 was again given the post of First Lord of the Admiralty. When Neville Chamberlain resigned after the failure of his appeasement policy Churchill became Prime Minister in May 1940.

He had a flair for public speaking, and his patriotic broadcasts helped keep up British morale during Britain`s 'darkest hours' in 1940–1.

What was done to protect children from bombing raids?

Even before war broke out, the British government had made plans to evacuate children from major cities to the safety of the countryside. It was widely expected that within days of the declaration of war German bombers would attack British cities. No one wanted children to be put at risk. Some parents took up the government's offer of sending their children to the USA, but this practice soon came to an end once German submarines began sinking passenger ships.

At the end of August 1939 the government began moving nearly two million children out of the danger areas. When the bombs didn't come many of the evacuees returned home. However, there had to be further evacuation in October 1940 at the start of the Blitz.

Often the bewildered evacuees had little idea what was happening to them. Parents did not always know where their children were going. The government told the parents that their children would be well looked after, and the worrying parents had to hope this was true.

The evacuation process was often a great shock to all concerned. The vast majority of children were from poor areas of the big cities. The country families who received them were sometimes shocked by just how deprived many of these children were. For some evacuees their time in the countryside was a pleasurable experience. For others it was a time of great unhappiness.

M SOURCE

A government poster from the Second World War.

L SOURCE

The government has made plans for the removal of schoolchildren from what are called 'evacuable' areas to safer places. Householders have offered homes where the children will be made welcome. The children will have their schoolteachers and other helpers with them. The transport of three million children is an enormous undertaking. It would not be possible to let all parents know in advance the place to where each child will be sent. Of course it means heartache to be separated from your children, but you can be quite sure that they will be well looked after.

From a government leaflet, 'Evacuation: Why and How?', 1939.

N SOURCE

Everything was so clean in the room. We were given face flannels and tooth brushes. We'd never cleaned our teeth until then. And hot water from a tap. And there was a lavatory upstairs. And carpets. And something called an eiderdown. And clean sheets. This was all very odd. I didn't like it. It was scary.

Memories of a Second World War evacuee.

SOURCE

The woman said, 'Here's your meal' and gave us a tin of pilchards between the two of us and some bread and water. Now we'd been in a rich woman's house before, so we said, 'Where's the butter?' And we got a sudden wallop round the head. What we later found out was that the woman hated kids and was doing it for the extra money. So the meals were the cheapest you could dish up.

Michael Caine, who later became a famous actor, remembers life as an evacuee.

Q

SOURCE

I thought it was a Sunday school outing down to the sea-side. And I looked out of the bus window and I saw my mother crying outside. I said to my brother, 'What's mummy crying for?' and my brother said, 'Shut up!'

Memories of a Second World War evacuee.

P

SOURCE

Children on their way to the countryside, 1938.

Caine

Although Michael Caine (1933–) is one of the most famous of Britain's living actors, he does not come from a wealthy family. He was born in the East End of London (his real name is Maurice Micklewhite). Shortly after the war broke out he was evacuated to the countryside. He was educated at Wilson's Grammar School in Peckham, London, and served in the army in Berlin and in Korea between 1951 and 1953. After his army service he worked in repertory theatres in Horsham and Lowestoft and thus spent years as a struggling actor, playing minor parts in theatre and television.

In 1963 he played the part of an officer in the film *Zulu*. His performance in that part launched a career that has taken in hundreds of films and plays. He has been nominated four times for an Academy Award and in 1986 won an Oscar for Best Supporting Actor in *Hannah and her Sisters*.

What other changes did the war bring for civilians?

During the war German bombing caused extensive damage to housing and other public buildings. Many parents worried about having their children looked after by strangers when they were evacuated to the countryside. But there were also other important changes in people's life-style.

Working women

One of the major changes affected women. During the war many women went out to work for the first time. In 1939 more than a million people had been unemployed. When war broke out, however, all men aged 18–41 were called up to do military service and so there was a shortage of labour. The government looked to women to fill the gap. In 1941 women under 50 (except those with young families) had to register for war work. Some took jobs in factories. Others joined the Women's Land Army and worked on farms. By 1943 three-quarters of single women or those with children over 14 were doing war work. For many women the war brought their first taste of independence. They had their own wage packets and were responsible for the household finances. This was a significant step towards creating a more equal society. Some women also volunteered to work as nurses, or as members of the Women's Voluntary Service – their work included running canteens in bombed-out areas and sending food parcels to the troops.

SOURCE S

The word 'mock' crept into the vocabulary. There was mock cream, mock hamburgers, mock potato omelette – with plenty of potato, but no eggs. Mock duck was a recipe of beans, lentils, and mashed potatoes, flavoured with sage and onion and 'shaped to look like a duck'.

Margaret Costa, 'The Food Front', in the 'Sunday Times', 1965.

SOURCE T

Most people are better fed than they used to be. There are less fat people. For instance, with the adult milk ration of three pints a week, the amount of milk being drunk has actually increased since the war started.

The author George Orwell commenting during the Second World War on the effects of rationing.

SOURCE R

A wartime painting showing a woman working as a skilled machinist.

76

Men who were not fit enough for military service or who were in **reserved occupations** (jobs such as coal mining which were vital for the war effort) could still play a part as a volunteer. In the Blitz many volunteers acted as fire-fighters, ambulance drivers and air-raid wardens. Some joined the **Home Guard** (now affectionately known as Dad's Army) which was a volunteer reserve army, in case of invasion.

Rationing

During the war, German submarines sank ships bringing food to Britain. This caused food shortages. On 8 January 1940 the government tried to ensure that food supplies were shared out fairly by introducing **rationing**. Families were issued with a **ration book** which allowed them to buy a weekly amount of rationed food. At first only bacon, ham, butter and sugar were rationed; soon almost all basic foodstuffs were on ration.

Although people with money could always get food on the **black market**, most people tried to 'make do'. There were some very clever ways to prepare dishes that looked like the real thing – like wedding cakes, where most of what was under the icing was cardboard! The government encouraged people to grow more food. It used slogans like '**Dig for Victory**' and characters such as '**Potato Pete**' and '**Dr Carrot**' appeared on posters.

Fear

Perhaps the hardest aspect of the Home Front was the non-stop worry. Many parents were separated from their children, and wives from husbands. There was the constant fear of hearing that a loved one had died in battle or was the victim of a German bombing raid. It was with these terrible worries always at the back of their minds that the civilian population tried to cope with the day-to-day problems of being at war.

Wartime women on a protest march, 1942.

Orwell

George Orwell (1903–50) (whose real name was Eric Blair) was an English writer who was born in Bengal in India and educated at Eton. He returned to India after completing his schooling and served for five years with the Indian Imperial Police in Burma from 1922 to 1927. He then returned to Europe and began writing under the name of George Orwell.

He fought in the Spanish Civil War on the side of the Republicans and was seriously wounded. During the Second World War he was war correspondent for the BBC and the *Observer* newspaper. Many of his books reflect his support for the idea of Socialism. However, Orwell was bitterly critical of the USSR and wrote *Animal Farm* as a satire about Stalin's government. Orwell's most famous work *1984* was published in 1949. The book expresses his vision of the future when government controls all aspects of human life.

How did governments keep up civilian morale during the war?

The art of presenting information to influence the way people think is called **propoganda**. The Nazi Party made excellent use of propaganda during the 1930s in Germany. They set up a Ministry of Enlightenment and Propaganda headed by Joseph Goebbels. It proved highly effective in portraying the Nazi Party as the saviours of Germany.

During the Second World War both the Allies and the Axis powers (Germany, Italy and Japan) used propaganda to keep up the morale of the people. Sometimes this propaganda was blatant, showing the enemy as evil or wicked. Sometimes it was much more subtle. Newspapers could be encouraged (or instructed) to carry stories that seemed simply factual, but contained a hidden message. Modern party political broadcasts use the same approach nowadays to win support for political parties.

Although there was no television during the war, both sides made films for cinema which were designed to show them in a good light. They also used radio stations to broadcast to the enemy. Not only were there official stations, such as the BBC and Radio Moscow, there were also some which were not what they appeared to be. Germany ran radio stations from within its borders that pretended to be French. Britain set up organizations which said that they were official German forces broadcasting stations. Both were used for propaganda purposes.

SOURCE

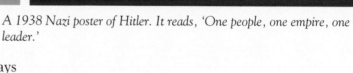

A 1938 Nazi poster of Hitler. It reads, 'One people, one empire, one leader.'

SOURCE

The parades, processions, demonstrations, ceremonies and rallies by which the Nazis impressed the German people were nearly all his idea. He shared Hitler's belief that if you tell a lie often enough it will be believed.

Description of Goebbels from C. Culpin, 'Making History', 1984.

BOMB CRASHES DOWN HOSPITAL STAIRS

Daily Express Raid Reporters

One of the oldest London hospitals was hit by a bomb last night. The bomb fell down the main staircase and shattered it – but none of the patients in the wards leading off the stairs was injured.

Only one person was injured – a member of the medical staff who was in a small room at the top of the building.

A volunteer fireman climbed a ladder and brought him down from the wreckage.

Ward sisters and doctors opened the doors after the explosion and found a hole in front of them where the staircase had been.

They at once organised a human chain to carry the patients down a fire escape to beds on the ground floor.

A member of the hospital staff said shortly afterwards: "The doctor who was injured is undergoing an operation. His condition is fair.

"Everything is under control, and we are still recieving patients.

"We had to turn off the water and gas, but we have a little in our tanks, and we can still deal with urgent cases."

This is the fifth hospital in London damaged by Nazi bombs. One has been attacked twice.

Last night the raiders appeared to fly over London two or three at a time at frequent intervals. They dropped bombs indiscriminately over a wide area

Extract from the 'Daily Express', 16 September 1940.

Goebbels

Joseph Goebbels (1897–1945) became famous as the man who organized German propaganda during the Second World War. He was born in the Rhineland, German, and in 1920 became a Doctor of Philosopher at Heidelberg University. In 1922 he joined the Nazi Party and was made Nazi leader of Berlin in 1926. From 1929 he was responsible for organizing Nazi propaganda and in 1930 was elected into the Reichstag. From 1933 to 1945 he held the post of Minister of Enlightenment and Propaganda. This gave him complete control over all forms of communication and expression within Germany. The press was controlled and art, music and literature censored. Goebbels became an expert on the use of radio to convey the Nazi message, and also organized huge rallies, the most spectacular of which were held at Nuremberg.

During the Second World War Goebbels urged the German people to make even greater efforts, but could not prevent Germany's defeat. When he realized that Nazi Germany could not survive he killed his wife and children, before committing suicide in Hitler's bunker.

We had become so accustomed to the explosive headlines, that we failed to grasp the full significance of the horror stories as they progressed from some humble position on the back page of the newspaper to blazing two-inch headlines on the front. 'Pregnant Sudeten German mother pushed off bicycle by Czech sub-human!'

Description of how Hitler used the newspapers as propaganda before invading the Sudetenland, Czechoslovakia in 1938.

A Russian cartoon from the Second World War.

5.1 A Divided Europe

The division of Europe after 1945.

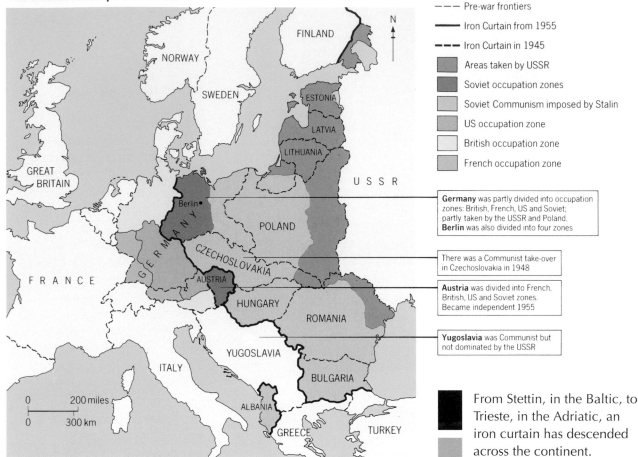

Legend:
- --- Pre-war frontiers
- — Iron Curtain from 1955
- --- Iron Curtain in 1945
- Areas taken by USSR
- Soviet occupation zones
- Soviet Communism imposed by Stalin
- US occupation zone
- British occupation zone
- French occupation zone

Germany was partly divided into occupation zones: British, French, US and Soviet; partly taken by the USSR and Poland. **Berlin** was also divided into four zones

There was a Communist take-over in Czechoslovakia in 1948

Austria was divided into French, British, US and Soviet zones. Became independent 1955

Yugoslavia was Communist but not dominated by the USSR

On 7 May 1945 the last German armies surrendered to the Allies. Hitler and Mussolini were both dead. On 17 July the victorious Allies met at **Potsdam** near Berlin. Here they agreed their arrangements for the running of Europe after the war. Earlier in 1945 they had met at **Yalta** in the Crimea and had made a number of important decisions. Germany would be split into four parts, or **zones**, with each zone controlled by one of the allies: Britain, the USA, France and USSR. **Berlin** would also be split into four zones, even though it lay deep in the Soviet zone of Germany. This was because it was the capital.

At Potsdam the Allies agreed that Poland would lose some of its eastern lands to the USSR and make up for this by being given part of Germany. A **United Nations Organization** would be set up to replace the League of Nations. There would be **free elections** in the countries liberated from the Nazis.

> From Stettin, in the Baltic, to Trieste, in the Adriatic, an iron curtain has descended across the continent.

Winston Churchill in a speech at Fulton, USA, in 1946.

> By 1948 all the countries which the USSR controlled had one party governments controlled by the Communists. The Red Army helped Communists take control of the police, the radio and the newspapers. They interfered with elections if they were going against them.

SOURCE

J. Scott, 'The World Since 1914', 1989.

Even before the Potsdam Conference, Stalin had arrested non-Communist politicians in **Poland**. He was determined to control the countries that he had captured from the Germans. Germans were forced out of Poland, Czechoslovakia and Hungary. They were forced to move to Germany. Thousands died on the way. In Germany the Allies, especially the USSR, seized factory machines to help pay for the war.

Now that Germany had been defeated it became clear just how little the Allies had in common. The western democracies thought that the Soviets intended to impose Communism on as many countries as they could, to become more powerful. In 1945 the USSR made sure Communists won the Bulgarian elections. In 1947 Communist governments took power in Hungary and Romania and crushed opposition in Poland. In 1948 they seized power in Czechoslovakia. Other Communists were in control of Yugoslavia and Albania. This frightened the western leaders.

In 1947 the President of the USA, **Truman**, made it clear that he would oppose any further spread of Communism. This became known as the **Truman Doctrine**. Europe was divided by politics and distrust. A **'Cold War'** was beginning.

C

SOURCE

As early as 1941 Stalin had made it clear that the USSR would only permit friendly countries on its borders. He remarked that twice in 30 years the USSR had been invaded through an unfriendly Poland.

L. Snellgrove, 'The Modern World Since 1870', 1981.

Tito

Josip Broz (1892–1980), known as Tito, became famous as leader of the Yugoslavian partisans during the Second World War. In the First World War he fought in the Austrian army and became a prisoner of war in Russia. He stayed to fight for the Bolsheviks (Communists) in the civil war. Tito returned to Yugoslavia in 1920, but was imprisoned for six years as a Communist agitator. In 1941 the Germans occupied Yugoslavia and Tito organized the resistance movement against them. At the end of the war he became Prime Minister of Yugoslavia. In 1953 he was made President and held that office until his death in1980.

D

SOURCE

Leading Nazis were put on trial for their 'war crimes'. The most famous trials were held in Nuremberg. Many of those responsible, though, were never brought to justice.

5.2 The United Nations Organization

In 1941 Churchill and Roosevelt made an agreement called the **Atlantic Charter**. In it they set out their aims: the British Empire should not gain any more colonies; countries liberated during the war should be free to run themselves; world living conditions should be improved; people should be free to travel; weapons of war should be reduced.

In January 1942, 26 nations signed the **Declaration of the United Nations**, which meant they agreed with the ideas of the Atlantic Charter. In 1944 Britain, China, the USA and the USSR began planning a new organization to encourage peaceful cooperation between countries. This would replace the failed League of Nations.

The idea was discussed again at the Allied meeting at Yalta in January 1945. In April, representatives of 50 nations met in San Francisco. After discussions they signed the **United Nations Charter** which set out the ideas of the new organization.

B

SOURCE

1 Oppose war.
2 Defend the dignity and worth of all people.
3 Uphold equal rights for men and women.
4 Uphold equal rights for all countries.
5 Respect treaties and International Law.
6 Improve standards of living in the world.

The main beliefs laid down in the United Nations Charter, 1945.

C

SOURCE

The League was created in the belief that all nations were fair and just and would put the good of the world before their own interests. The UN accepts that nations are greedy, selfish, and prepared to help only as long as too much is not demanded of them. The UN has not made the mistake of pretending that all nations are equal but recognizes that major powers must have more say in world decisions than small nations.

P. Moss, 'Modern World History', 1978.

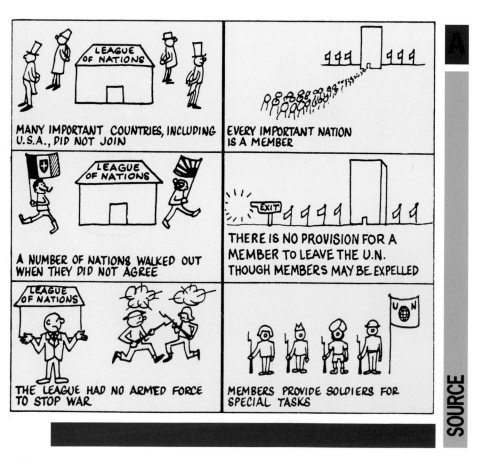

A

SOURCE

Comparing the UN and the League, from P. Moss, 'History Alive', 1977.

The UN is organized differently from the League of Nations. The representatives of member countries meet in the **General Assembly**. A two-thirds majority is needed to agree a decision. Most decisions are in the hands of a **Security Council**. In 1945 this had five permanent members (Britain, China, France, USA, USSR) and six temporary members. The number of temporary members was increased to ten after 1965. Each temporary member is only on the Council for two years.

The Security Council meets throughout the year and its decisions apply to all members of the UN. The permanent members have the **right of veto**. This means that if one of them votes against an idea, that idea cannot be passed. The aim of this was to make sure that any decision had the support of all the major countries of the world.

The Security Council has a large group of people to carry out its decisions. Their work is overseen by the **Secretary General**. The first was a Norwegian, **Trygve Lie**.

The United Nations Organization has set up a huge number of different committees and agencies to carry out its work. These include the **Court of International Justice**, which was taken over from the League of Nations; the **Food and Agriculture Organization (FAO)** which helps improve farming and protect natural resources; the **UN Education, Scientific and Cultural Organization (UNESCO)** which encourages education and understanding between nations; the **World Health Organization (WHO)** helping to improve world health; the **UN Relief and Rehabilitation Administration (UNRRA)** and the **International Refugee Organization (IRO)** which helps refugees.

At the end of the war the UN also played a part in helping to organize loans to countries to help them rebuild their economies again.

SOURCE

The League failed for two reasons. First, powerful countries like the USA and Germany after 1933 were not members. Second, it could only ask members to take action to keep peace.

The UN avoided the first of these weaknesses. All the Allies agreed to join and later on so did the defeated countries. But the second weakness was harder to avoid. Governments were not likely to give up national power by letting the new world organization have much power of its own.

J. Scott, 'The World Since 1914', 1989.

Hammarskjöld

Dag Hammarskjöld (1905–61) was a Professor of Economics at Stockholm University in Sweden and a member of the Swedish government, before becoming a delegate to the United Nations (UN). When the first UN Secretary-General, Trygve Lie, retired in 1953 Hammarskjöld took his place. He was re-elected to the post in 1957. Hammarskjöld had many problems to deal with during his time as Secretary-General, and won great support for his determination to show that the UN could play a significant role in helping to maintain world peace. In 1956 there was a serious crisis in the Middle East when the British invaded Egypt and took over the Suez Canal. Hammarskjöld played a major part in persuading the British to withdraw. After this he made many attempts to find a peaceful solution to the problems in the Middle East. In 1960–61 serious fighting broke out in the Belgian Congo. Hammarskjöld flew to Africa to try to resolve the dispute. He was killed when his plane crashed over Zambia.

5.3 Refugees

Refugees are people who have been forced to leave their homes. This can be because of war, or some kind of natural disaster. During the twentieth century many thousands of people have become refugees as a result of warfare. At the end of the Second World War hundreds of thousands of people found themselves without a home.

Many people had their homes destroyed by fighting and were forced to escape with the few belongings that they could carry. Others were forced to leave their homes because they were hated because of their nationality. Jews who survived the Nazi extermination camps often ended up thousands of miles from their original homes. Between 1945 and 1947 the liberated countries of eastern Europe expelled over 16 million Germans who lived in their countries. One in eight died as they were forced to flee westward. During the war the Germans and Japanese had made thousands of people work as **forced labour**. When the war ended these people were left far from home. In Japan, US bombing had destroyed thousands of homes. In China the war had disrupted civilian life for eight years. All these refugees were in danger from hunger, cold, disease and the cruelty of other people.

As early as 1943 the western Allies set up plans for helping refugees. They set up the **International Refugee Organization** and later the **United Nations Relief and Rehabilitation Administration (UNRRA)**. They worked behind the front lines and continued their work when the war ended. They provided temporary homes in Refugee Camps and food and clothing. They helped people get back to where their homes had been, or set up a new life elsewhere. Much of the money to do this work was provided by the USA. After the war, in 1947, the Americans provided even more money to help rebuild the economies of countries wrecked by the war. This was called **Marshall Aid**. As well as providing help, the USA aimed to stop the spread of communism into these countries.

The evidence in this unit explains why so many people were made refugees as a result of the Second World War and what life was like for some of these men, women and children.

A **SOURCE**

Berlin is a city of desolation and shattered dreams, inhabited by a half mad, half starving population, clawing its way into battered food shops, slinking for shelter into cellars and begging favours from the victors.

Soviet officer, 1945.

B **SOURCE**

Sowing of crops in many battle stricken areas is impossible this year. The food production will, for some time, be below the pre-war level.

Statement by representatives of Britain, USA and Canada following the Washington Conference on Problems of World Supplies and Distribution, 30 April 1945.

C **SOURCE**

Millions of Germans, Danzigers and Sudetenlanders are now on the move. Groups will take to the road, trek hundreds of miles and lose half their numbers through disease or exhaustion.

'Manchester Guardian', November 1945.

Chinese refugees in 1946.

Marshall

George Marshall (1880–1959) was a US army officer and statesman. He was Army Chief of Staff in the Second World War and Secretary of State in Truman's government after the war. He strongly supported Truman's anti-communist policy and thought that Communism flourished best where there was poverty and suffering. Because much of Europe was suffering the economic effects of world war, he thought there was a danger that Communism would take root. It was, therefore, the duty of the USA to provide economic aid. As Marshall himself said in 1947, 'The truth of the matter is that Europe's requirements for the next three or four years are so much greater than her present ability to pay that she must have substantial help.'

Marshall therefore devised the Marshall Plan which mad e available $15,000 million in aid for post-war reconstruction. Sixteen nations took advantage of the aid that the USA was offering. As a result of this plan Marshall was awarded the Nobel Peace Prize in 1953.

E

Throughout history, warfare has led to the mistreatment of those civilians unfortunate enough to live within the areas of fighting. Often villages were destroyed and civilians slaughtered; sometimes the fighting disrupted food production and the civilians starved to death. The Second World War, however, brought changes in the way that warfare was conducted. From now on civilians would increasingly become targets for attack. The Blitz, the Allied bombing of Germany and the US air raids on Japan, took a terrible toll in human lives.

In addition came the losses through disease, starvation and homelessness.

N. Kelly, *'The Second World War'*, 1989.

F

The Japanese occupied vast areas of the Far East and their treatment of native populations was relatively humane. But Hitler's Third Reich based its economy on the employment of slave labour in the factories, mines and on the land. Thus in the Second World War the Germans were responsible for shifting many nationalities all over Europe. There was little happiness for 'refugees' and 'displaced persons'. Some fled westwards to escape the advancing Red Army; others, liberated by British and US troops, tried to find their way home.

B. Catchpole, *'A Map History of the Modern World'*, 1982.

5.4 The End of Empires

At the beginning of the Second World War European countries such as Britain, France, Portugal, Belgium and the Netherlands controlled large empires. These were mostly made up of land (**colonies**) captured in Africa and in Asia. Within twenty years of 1945 almost all these colonies had become independent. The European empires had collapsed. Why did this happen?

These European powers were all **democracies**. But they would not allow the people living in their colonies a full say in how their countries were run. **Nationalist movements** in the colonies grew in strength as a result of the war. Members of the nationalist movements wanted their countries to be independent and free to run their own governments. The colonies also did not like the European powers taking raw materials.

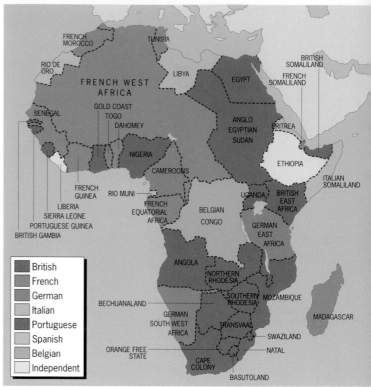

Africa in 1900

The war itself had encouraged the demand for independence. During the war European colonies in Asia had been taken over by the Japanese. The land was only recaptured with difficulty. While the Japanese had come to be hated by most of the people that they conquered, they had shown that the mighty European nations could be beaten. This made it impossible for countries such as **France** simply to retake its lands in **Indo-China** or the **Netherlands** to rebuild its empire in **Indonesia**. The people were no longer ready to accept the return of European rule. The European nations were defeated.

During the war with the Japanese in Asia, the colonial countries had gained experience in fighting. They could now use these skills to fight the returning European armies. They used **guerrilla tactics** to fight for freedom. This meant ambushing the enemy in small groups, rather than fighting full-pitch battles. The European countries found it hard to resist these struggles for independence because they were exhausted from the long fight against both the Germans and the Japanese.

SOURCE

[In 1914] India was valued as a market for British goods, especially cotton, a source of soldiers for the British army and for the prestige brought by it being a British colony.

W. O. Simpson, 'Changing Horizons, 1986'.

SOURCE

To have stayed in India for a moment longer would have broken Britain financially and militarily.

Lord Ismay, 'The Memoirs of Lord Ismay', 1960. India gained its independence from Britain in 1947.

In 1947 Britain gave up its Indian Empire. Since 1919 there had been a strong movement within India to gain independence. The British could no longer resist the force of this pressure. Two new countries emerged – **India and Pakistan**. The French fought a terrible war between 1948 and 1954 to try to retake **Indochina**. They failed and the result was the emergence of the new and independent countries of **North Vietnam, South Vietnam, Laos** and **Cambodia**. The Dutch attempt to regain Indonesia failed by 1949. During the 1960s most of the countries controlled by European countries in Africa gained independence. The first to do so was **Libya** in 1951. The Portugese kept **Angola** and **Mozambique** until 1975 but by then the other European countries had given independence to their African colonies. They had accepted that they could no longer control the freedom of the people of Africa and Asia.

D SOURCE

Fifteen years ago nationalism swept through Asia as countries pressed to be independent. Today, the wind of change is blowing through Africa. We must all accept it as a fact.

Harold Macmillan, the British Prime Minister, speaking to the South African parliament in February 1960.

C SOURCE

The Indonesians had been successful partly because of the anti-colonial feeling which won them sympathy from other countries and support from the United Nations; partly because the Netherlands was a small, far away country weakened by the Second World War and partly because enough Indonesians were prepared to fight and die to make the Dutch position impossible.

'History of the Twentieth Century', 1968, explaining why the Netherlands failed to retake part of its empire in Asia.

Attlee

Clement Attlee (1883–1967) was Prime Minister of Britain from 1945-51. He lectured at the London School of Economics before joining the army and fighting in the First World War. In 1922 he became a Labour MP. He was deputy prime minister in Churchill's wartime government and after the war became Prime Minister, following Labour's landslide victory in 1945. His government introduced the National Health Service and granted independence to India.

E SOURCE

VERSTERKT ONZE GELEDEREN

KONINKLIJK NEDERLANDSCH INDISCH LEGER

A Dutch army poster. It is aimed at recruiting soldiers to keep the Dutch colony in Indonesia. The Dutch had to agree to the Indonesians getting independence in December 1949.

5.5 The Beginnings of the Cold War

Since 1917 the USSR had been a communist country. Land, factories, transport systems and businesses were taken over by the government. This was because the communists believed that profits should be shared amongst all the people. The workers were supposed to be in control. But Stalin, who governed the USSR after the death of Lenin, proved to be an even harsher ruler than Tsar Nicholas had been. The USA and Western Europe was capitalist and democratic. Almost all land, factories and businesses were owned by individuals who ran them to make a profit from the capital they had invested. The government was elected by the people who were free to criticize it.

In the years immediately after the Second World War the USSR had been responsible for the spread of communism throughout Eastern Europe. The USA felt that the USSR had won the right to have a say about what happened in Eastern Europe, after the horrors of the Nazi invasion. But the USA also wanted free elections there and to be able to trade with east European countries. The Soviets feared that this American opposition would eventually lead to an attack on the USSR to destroy communism. Consequently, two countries which had previously been allies against Nazi Germany found themselves in bitter opposition.

This confrontation became known as the **Cold War**. It involved not only the USA and the USSR, but also their allies in western and eastern Europe. There was no direct fighting, but instead a war of words where each side used propaganda to try to score diplomatic victories by discrediting the other side`s actions. The Cold War was based on suspicion and mistrust.

B

SOURCE

At the present moment in world history nearly every nation must chose between two alternative ways of life. One way of life is based upon the will of the majority, and is distinguished by free institutions, representative government and free elections. The second way of life is based upon the will of the minority forcibly imposed upon terror and oppression and the suppression of personal freedom.

Part of President Truman's speech in 1947, setting out the Truman Doctrine.

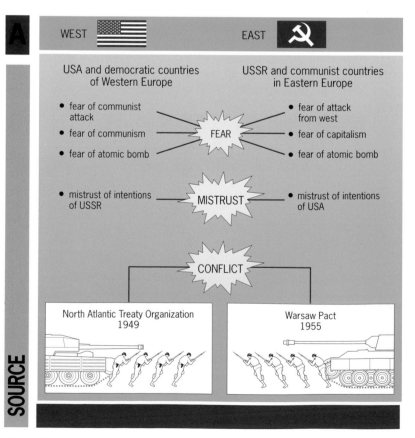

A

SOURCE

The Cold War: The product of fear.

In 1947 President Truman promised that the USA would give help to any country, anywhere in the world, which felt threatened by communism. This **Truman Doctrine** was quickly followed by the **Marshall Plan**, which promised financial assistance to countries needing help to repair war damage. Western Europe had suffered heavy damage in the war and needed rebuilding. The USA offered large sums of money in aid to western European countries. This would help these countries regain their strength and enable them to resist the threat of communism. The Truman Doctrine and Marshall Plan were part of an American policy called **containment**. In effect the USA was using economic aid to fight a war against communism.

Soviet fears that the USA intended to destroy the USSR were reinforced in 1949 when the Americans helped form the **North Atlantic Treaty Organization** (NATO). This was a formal military alliance of ten European countries plus Canada and the USA. In response, in 1955, the USSR linked the countries of eastern Europe together into a military alliance called the **Warsaw Pact**.

The climate of suspicion meant that each side had to be prepared for the possibility of military warfare breaking out. Both the USSR and the USA spent huge sums on developing their armies and weapons in preparation for any military conflict which might take place. By 1964 the two sides had over 3000 nuclear missiles between them. This was enough to destroy the world many times over.

A Soviet poster accusing the Americans of developing chemical weapons. The three barrels are labelled 'The Plague, Cholera, and Typhus'. At the front of the vehicle the American Secretary of State is saying to the Secretary-General of the United Nations, 'The USA does not use chemical weapons.'

Truman

Harry S. Truman (1884–1972) was the USA's 33rd President. He is particularly famous for authorizing the dropping of the atomic bombs on Hiroshima and Nagasaki.

In 1935 Truman was elected Senator for the State of Missouri. When Roosevelt won the 1944 Presidential election, Truman was his Vice-President and took office when Roosevelt died in 1945. He was re-elected in 1948 in a surprise victory over Thomas Dewey. In 1952 he refused to stand again for office.

C

SOURCE

5.6 From Confrontation to Co-operation

In July 1955 there was a 'thaw' in the Cold War when the leaders of the USA, the USSR, Britain, France and China met in Geneva. It was hoped that this might lead to **peaceful co-existence** between nations instead of continued mistrust. But events soon dashed any such hopes.

- In 1956 Hungary tried to carry out reforms and leave the Warsaw Pact. The USSR reacted by invading Hungary and executing the Hungarian Prime Minister. The West was horrified at the harshness of the Soviet reaction.

- As relations worsened so the USSR decided to block the only 'hole in the Iron Curtain'. It was still possible to cross the Iron Curtain by travelling from East to West Berlin. Between 1949 and 1961 more than 2.5 million East Berliners crossed into the West. From the morning of 13 August 1961 this was no longer possible. The USSR had begun to build the Berlin Wall. Between 1961 and 1962, 41 East Germans lost their lives trying to cross the Berlin Wall and for almost 40 years it was the symbol of the Cold War.

- In 1962 the world was brought to the brink of nuclear war when the USSR and the USA clashed over the Caribbean island of Cuba. American spy planes showed that the Cuban leader, Fidel Castro, was allowing the Soviets to build missile bases on the island. This put 80 million Americans within range of Soviet missiles.

A **SOURCE**

The steel-shod Soviet jackboot heeled down on Hungary this week, stamping and grinding out the young democracy in Hungary.

Comment on the USSR's invason of Hungary in the American magazine, 'Time'.

B **SOURCE**

The minutes ticked slowly by. It was 10.25 a.m. A messenger brought in a note, 'Mr President, we have a note that the Soviet ships have stopped and turned round.'

Robert Kennedy, the President's brother, remembers when the news came that the world would not be going to war, during the Cuban Missile crisis of 1962.

The threat to the USA from Soviet missile on Cuba.

C **SOURCE**

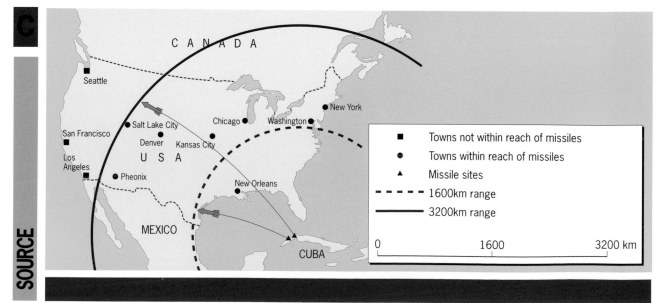

Legend:
- ■ Towns not within reach of missiles
- ● Towns within reach of missiles
- ▲ Missile sites
- - - - 1600km range
- —— 3200km range

0   1600   3200 km

The President of the USA, John F. Kennedy, was informed that the Soviets were sending ships to Cuba loaded with nuclear missiles. Kennedy could not tolerate this threat to American security and used warships to blockade Cuba and prevent Soviet ships from reaching the island. If the Soviet ships did not stop they would be boarded by the Americans – and war would probably follow. As the world held its breath the news came that the Soviet ships had stopped and turned round. As a result of the crisis the USA and the USSR set up a 'hot line' teleprinter link between Washington and Moscow to prevent any further 'misunderstandings'.

- After 1962 there was a slight improvement in relations. Then, in 1968, there was a rising in **Czechoslovakia** against rule from Moscow. The USSR invaded and ruthlessly crushed the revolt. Once again, the mistrust between the USA and USSR was increased. From time to time talks were held to see if each side would agree to reduce their stockpiles of nuclear arms. Little progress was made.

In 1985 **Mikhail Gorbachev** came to power in the USSR. He set out to improve relations with the West and improve living conditions at home. His open approach, however, had the effect of encouraging people in east European countries to question being controlled from Moscow. They demanded independence and democracy.

Dramatic events followed in 1989. One by one communist governments in eastern Europe were brought down. The hated Berlin Wall was torn down and, in 1990, Germany was reunified as a single country. The Cold War was over. More drama followed inside the USSR. In November 1991 the Communist Party was overthrown. One month later the USSR was disbanded and Gorbachev was forced to resign.

Khrushchev

Nikita Sergeyevich Khrushchev (1874–91) was leader of the Soviet Union from 1953–64. He came from a farming background and did not learn to read or write until he was 25. When Stalin died in 1953 he became First Secretary of the Communist Party. After his defeat in the Cuban Missile Crisis he was deposed in 1964.

1989: The end of the Warsaw Pact

5 June:	Communist Party defeated in Polish elections.
10 Sept:	Hungary opens border with Austria. Thousands flee.
1 Oct:	Czechoslovakia opens borders. Thousands flee.
9 Nov:	Berlin Wall is breached in East Germany.
10 Nov:	Bulgarian communist dictator, Zhikov, overthrown.
24 Nov:	Czech Communist Party leaders resign.
22 Dec:	Romanian dictator, Ceausescu, overthrown and executed.

How communism came to an end in eastern Europe.

SOURCE D

A happy crowd help tear up the Berlin Wall in November 1989.

6.1 The Changing World

At the end of the 20th century increasing numbers of people are living to the age of one hundred. In their lifetime the world has experienced rapid changes, which few people could even have dreamt of at the end of the last century.

Communications

The development of transport has brought about a significant change in the lives of many people. In 1900 it was unusual for people to make long journeys and little was known about other countries. There were no cars or aeroplanes and travel could be both difficult and tiresome. For example, a journey by ocean liner to America took five days. Today the same journey by air takes a matter of hours. All countries in the world can now be reached in a single day from any part of the world. The growth in car ownership has been rapid. There are well over 400 million cars in the world and this number is increasing all the time.

There has also been a revolution in communications. Modern telephone systems allow people to be in instant touch with any part of the world. Facsimile (fax) machines have made it possible to send letters and pictures thousands of miles in a matter of seconds.

These developments have led to the **shrinking world** as our knowledge of other countries increases and the rate at which we receive this information accelerates. This process has been

A SOURCE

Boeing 747s in flight.

B SOURCE

More and more people now own television sets and video recorders.

helped by **computer technology** which enables newspapers to print stories on the same day they happen. There has also been an incredible increase in the ownership of radios and televisions. In the USA in 1945 there were 10,000 television sets in use; in the late 20th century this had risen to over 140 million. The development of **satellite technology** means that pictures can be beamed across the world as they happen.

Medicine and engineering

Medical science has also advanced. **High-technology medicine** means it is now possible to carry out liver, kidney and heart transplants. This does not mean to say, however, that traditional forms of medicine (such as faith-healing and acupuncture) have disappeared or that medical science has conquered everything. For example, there is still no cure for cancer or AIDS.

Advances in engineering mean that we can build huge cities with impressive skyscrapers and huge tunnels such as the one under the Channel which links Britain and France. Labour saving devices in the house, such as washing machines, vacuum cleaners, dishwashers and microwave ovens have also helped create more leisure time.

Continuing Poverty

Yet it would be wrong to think that these advances have made everyone more knowledgeable and brought about a better standard of living for all. In many of the world's developing countries people live on the edge of starvation and appear to have benefited little from technological advances elsewhere. Even within the developed countries of the world there is great variety in the standards of living. Whilst many people have high standards of living, increasing numbers are having to deal with problems caused by unemployment and poverty.

Whether developments in arms technology are progress is also arguable. Has the development of nuclear weapons so frightened countries that we will never have another world war? Or has it just created a nightmare situation where the next war will destroy the world?

SOURCE

Britain and the Undeveloped World in 1991				
Country	GDP per capita (in US dollars)	Literacy Rate	Life Expectancy Male	Female
Britain	16,750	99%	73	79
Ethiopia	120	66%	43	49
Laos	230	84%	50	53
Bangladesh	220	35%	53	53
Haiti	370	53%	55	58
Yemen	540	39%	52	52

GDP stands for 'Gross Domestic Product'. This is the total value of the goods and services produced in a year. In this case it has been divided by the number of people living in each country to give the value of goods produced by each person. GDP is one way of comparing life in different countries.

SOURCE

Many hundreds of people in the the poorer countries are preoccupied solely with survival and elementary needs. For them work is frequently not available, or when it is, pay is very low and conditions often barely tolerable. Homes are constructed of impermanent materials and have neither piped water nor sanitation. In the developed countries ordinary men and women face genuine economic problems - uncertainty, inflation, the fear of not the reality of unemployment. But they rarely face anything resembling the total deprivation of the under-developed countries.

Extract from the 'Brandt Report' written in 1980. Brandt was the ex-leader of West Germany who was commissioned to carry out an investigation by members of both developed and undeveloped countries.

Air pollution in Los Angeles, California, USA.

The environment

Technological advance has also had a bad effect on our environment. Industry is rapidly using up the world`s natural resources and at the same time causing environmental pollution. Many of our cities suffer from smog (a mixture of smoke, fumes and fog) which help produce bronchitis and even lung cancer. Environmentalists continue to debate the dangers to our ozone layer and the potential effects of global warming. At the same time acid rain is wiping out forests and poisoning lakes in countries such as Sweden. Nuclear power carries with it even greater dangers. In 1986 a nuclear reactor exploded in **Chernobyl** in USSR. The radioactive material which escaped will continue to cause death and sickness for many years to come.

As the century draws to a close there is growing concern for the environment and greater government involvement in trying to prevent damage to the planet. Solutions to the problem, however, are not easy. The prevention of further pollution will almost certainly harm countries' economies, increase unemployment and lower the standard of living of the wealthiest countries in the world.

Political changes

The late 1980s saw the beginning of dramatic changes in world politics. Communist governments began to collapse in eastern Europe. In 1989 the **Berlin Wall** came down and East and West Germany were reunited to make one democratic country. Yet just five years earlier these events would have been unthinkable. The person who unwittingly started this trend was **Mikhail Gorbachev**, who became the leader of the USSR in 1985. Events have also happened swiftly in South Africa. In 1990 **Nelson Mandela**, the anti-apartheid campaigner, was released from prison. The policy of apartheid was scrapped and black people were given equal voting rights. In 1994 Mandela became the first black president of South Africa. Just a few years earlier these happenings would have been unthinkable.

Europe is moving towards integration. The **European Union** is growing larger and creating a large amount of debate. Should there be one common currency? Will the individual members of the EU lose their own Parliaments and be totally ruled from Brussels? These are questions which remain unanswered.

Mandela

Nelson Rolihala Mandela (1918–) was born in Transkei in South Africa and trained as a lawyer. After the Second World War Mandela was one of the Black political leaders who formed the African National Congress. This body campaigned against apartheid in South Africa and advocated non-violent protest by the Black community. Mandela was arrested and imprisoned in 1964. Under the apartheid system Black people were not allowed to vote or become MPs. Following intense pressure from the international community Mandela was finally released in 1990. After the abolition of apartheid in 1994 Mandela was elected the first Black President of South Africa.

F

SOURCE

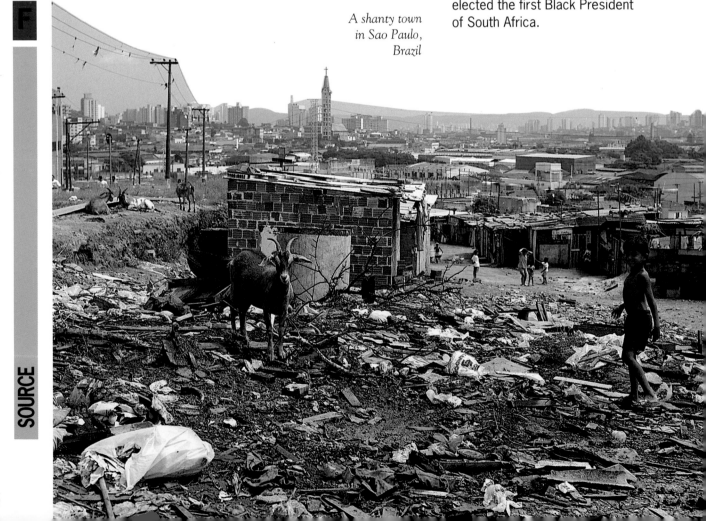

A shanty town in Sao Paulo, Brazil